Authentic Recipes from
Santa Fe

Recipes by Dave DeWitt and Nancy Gerlach
Photography by Eduardo Fuss
Styling by Christina Ong

PERIPLUS

Published by Periplus Editions, with editorial offices at
130 Joo Seng Road #06-01, Singapore 368357.
Tel: (65) 6280-1330 Fax: (65) 6280-6290
Email: inquiries@periplus.com.sg
Website: www.periplus.com

Distributed by

North America, Latin America and Europe
Tuttle Publishing, 364 Innovation Drive,
North Clarendon, VT 05759-9436.
Tel: (802) 773-8930 Fax: (802) 773-6993
Email: info@tuttlepublishing.com
www.tuttlepublishing.com

Japan
Tuttle Publishing, Yaekari Building 3F,
5-4-12 Osaki, Shinagawa-ku, Tokyo 141-0032.
Tel: (03) 5437-0171 Fax: (03) 5437-0755
Email: tuttle-sales@gol.com

Asia Pacific
Berkeley Books Pte Ltd.
130 Joo Seng Road #06-01
Singapore 368357.
Tel: (65) 6280-1330 Fax: (65) 6280-6290
Email: inquirics@pcriplus.com.sg
www.periplus.com

All recipes were tested in the Periplus Test Kitchen.

Photo credits: The painting on the cover is by
Amanda Grogan.

Acknowledgments:
The publisher would like to thank Robert Shure,
Marie Romero Cash, Peggy Jackson, Robin Ann
Powell, Rosalea Murphy, Christy Teetor, Emilio Romero,
Jr., Gregory Lomayesva and Heidi Loewen for their
generosity and their willingness to open their homes
and studios to us; Jose L. Villegas, Sr. at the State
Records Center and Archives and the staff at the
Palace of Governors; and Denice Skrepcinski for her
invaluable help in preparing the food for photography. A very special thank you to Paula Summers who
helped in innumerable ways and to Mrs Ong for her
culinary expertise and eye for detail, and to the many
chefs and artists for their enthusiastic participation in
this project. And to the people of Santa Fe, a big
thank you for their warmth and hospitality.

Contents

Food in Santa Fe

The "City Different" melds local traditions with a hip, modern style

In just a few short decades, Santa Fe has become the magical city of the Southwest, a destination for artists, writers, chefs and of course, tourists. Nicknamed The City Different, Santa Fe's reputation for tolerating individuality has had much to do with its attraction as a place to live. Its tremendous appeal as a trendy place to visit is the result of countless articles and books about the landscape, the art scene, the cuisine, the architecture and the Santa Fe look—in clothing and jewelry—all part of what is termed Santa Fe style. And though its overexposure has fostered a certain Santa Fe blasé, there is just no denying the incredible charm of the place.

The city is on a high desert mesa at seven thousand feet above sea level, offering spectacular views of the Sangre de Cristo Mountains that tower above it. The sun always seems to shine in Santa Fe and the quality of the light and the beauty of the mesas have drawn artists to the city for decades. The city's adobe architecture, unchanged for centuries, reveals Santa Fe's deep Native American roots. The buildings in the historic district—even new ones—all share the same ocher color and smooth mud finish.

Santa Fe residents view the huge influx of tourists each year as just a continuation of history. After all, during the past four hundred years Sante Fe has been controlled by Native Americans, Spaniards, Mexicans, Americans and Confederates. Each of these groups helped create the flavors of Santa Fe.

The first food fusion of Santa Fe occurred when Spanish settlers from Mexico founded the city in 1598, bringing European and Mexican ingredients that were combined with the corn cuisine of the native Pueblo Indians. New Mexican cuisine can thus be viewed as the northernmost of the Mexican regional cuisines; it is also the spiciest because of the New Mexicans' love of chile peppers. The second food fusion occurred when Anglo-Americans arrived with new ingredients, recipes and restaurants offering the standard meat and potatoes of the eastern United States. But what has really placed Santa Fe on the culinary map has occurred during the last twenty-five years: a proliferation of fine restaurants that have vastly expanded the concept of Southwestern cooking.

Many of Santa Fe's restaurants are the epitome of the concept of fusion, offering dishes that bridge the culinary gaps between cultures. Despite the international flavors, traditions are still strong. In homes and restaurants, visitors will still discover the delicious New Mexican dishes that depend upon the most basic New World ingredients: corn, beans, squash and chile peppers.

Native Americans and Their Food

When the first Spanish explorers ventured north from Mexico City in the sixteenth century and wandered into what is now the American Southwest, they encountered the descendants of a great prehistoric civilization, the Anasazi. These Native Americans, known as the Pueblo Indians, were clustered along the Rio Grande near present-day Santa Fe in separate villages, or pueblos. They made excellent use of nearly every edible animal and plant substance imaginable. For protein, the Native Americans hunted and trapped deer, rabbits, quail, pronghorn, bison and many other mammals and birds. The meat of this game was usually grilled over coals or added to a pot and turned into a stew.

However, some tribes (such as the Apaches) had taboos against eating certain animals that they regarded as repulsive: snakes, fish and owls, for example. Later on, after the appearance of European food animals, game was viewed as "poor man's meat." Today, of course, game has made a comeback because of its exotic nature and appeal to adventurous diners.

ABOVE: Corn is held sacred by Native Americans and has been an important part of the Southwestern diet for centuries. The rich colors of this Indian corn only appear once the corn has dried; when it is fresh the corn is a more subdued yellow or white.

The food plants eaten by the Native Americans were divided into two categories: those harvested in the wild and those cultivated plants that had managed to adapt to the dry desert climate or were irrigated. Harvested wild plants included acorns (from which flour was made), berries such as chokecherry and juniper, yucca fruits, various herbs such as wild mint, mushrooms, mesquite seeds (sometimes called beans) and agave hearts (mescal), which were roasted in pits by the Mescalero Apaches and other tribes. Three other wild crops were very important in Native American cooking (and are most commonly used today): cacti, piñon nuts and chiltepíns (wild, berrylike chile peppers). The cactus fruits and leaves were usually eaten raw, as in salads, while the piñon nuts were usually mixed with honey as a snack or dessert. Chiltepíns were used as a pungent spice before the Spanish introduced domesticated chiles.

Even though wild crops were important, the ancient Anasazi culture of the Southwest—and later the Pueblo Indians—depended on some important domesticated crops: corn, beans, squash and (after the Spanish arrived) chile peppers. It is not a coincidence that these foods are the foundation of Southwestern cuisine. Although domesticated in Mexico and Central America, these crops had moved north to what is now New Mexico long before the Spanish arrived.

Here in New Mexico we not only claim the oldest regional cuisine in the United States but continue to enjoy many of the foods that have been part of the Native American diet for hundreds or even thousands of years. Despite the influences of these ingredients, Native American cuisine these days has mostly been incorporated into what has become New Mexican cuisine, so wild plants and game are no longer as common as they once were.

Corn is so important to Native Americans that it serves as the basis of the cuisine and also plays a pivotal role in their religion and many of their ceremonies. The four kinds of corn—yellow, white, red and blue—were a gift from the gods or creator who taught the people how to plant, harvest, and use it before they were allowed to walk Mother Earth.

Beans, domesticated ten thousand years ago in Peru, even predate cultivated corn. Easy to grow and store, beans quickly became an essential part of the Native American diet. The Hopi grow fourteen kinds of beans in a variety of colors, which when combined with corn provide a complete protein source for times when game is scarce. Chile, another staple in the diet, was domesticated in both South and Central America about the same time as beans and also migrated north. And although there is little doubt that domesticated chile was introduced to Native Americans

OPPOSITE: The Deer Dance at San Juan Pueblo, which takes place in February, is performed by the young people of the tribe to honor the deer for the many gifts he has given them. The profile of a deer dancer is the symbol of the San Juan Pueblo people.

the Europeans is blue corn bread; undoubtedly, there was an earlier form of it that lacked the baking powder and milk used today. It is made with flour from Indian blue corn, and its brilliant blue color can be disconcerting to those not accustomed to it.

Other dishes likely to be encountered at the pueblos are fried red chiles, dried pods that are simply fried in lard or oil and eaten; green chile stew, which is virtually identical to the Hispanic version; green pumpkin stew, which is pumpkin stewed with corn, onions, green chiles and garlic; and red chile stew, which is usually made with pork.

Since meat was preserved in the old days by either salting or drying, an Indian favorite is beef or lamb jerky, which is often treated with chile powder. The jerky may be added to stews if fresh meat is not available.

The Spanish Contribution

Imagine Southwestern cuisine without beef, lamb, pork, chicken, cilantro, cumin, limes, garlic, onions, wheat bread, rice, beer and wine. That's where New World cooking would be without the Old. The Spanish colonists brought a new dimension to this ancient cuisine because the native people had never before experienced food sources such as cattle and wheat. The new foodstuffs merged with the old but did not overwhelm them. Rather, they were incorporated into the ancient techniques, and the result was a unique and highly spiced cuisine.

The Spaniards who first settled in Santa Fe brought with them the seeds to plant the crops they needed as well as livestock. Since Santa Fe was the terminus of the 1,500-mile-long Camino Real (Royal Road) from Mexico City, it became a trading center and both the beginning and the end for caravans of wagons. The Plaza in Santa Fe was where the wagons unloaded and vigorous trading was done in foodstuffs.

The primary crops of the colonists were corn and squash. Historian Marc Simmons wrote about the early Spanish agriculture: "Other field crops included the frijol beans, horsebeans, peas, squashes and pumpkins, melons, chile, tobacco and cotton. Only a limited variety of garden vegetables seem to have been cultivated in the later Colonial period. Onions and garlic were regarded as staples in the diet, but other things, such as cucumbers, lettuce, beets and the small husk-tomato, are mentioned in the documents only rarely. The potato was practically unknown."

The first and most important Old World influences were meats and grains. "Wherever Spaniards went, they took their livestock with them," notes John C. Super, an expert on colonial Latin American history. "Pigs, sheep and cattle were as much a part of the conquest as Toledo steel and fighting mastiffs."

LEFT: Making ristras, strings of chile peppers, by hand at the Rancho de las Golondrinas, which was a stopping place for caravans from Mexico and is now a living history museum.

of the Southwest by the Spaniards, there is evidence that at least the wild chiltepín was already growing in the Southwest when the Spaniards arrived.

One way to get a feel of the life of Native Americans and a taste of their version of New Mexican cuisine is to visit a pueblo. In the fall, with chile sun-drying on roofs or hung in strings (ristras) and corn stacked around the pueblo to dry, it is almost like stepping back in time. Occasionally, visitors are invited into homes for some food. Many of the dishes, such as enchiladas and tamales, show a Hispanic influence, but there are a few specialties that are uniquely Indian. Interestingly enough, most Indian dishes today are made with ingredients imported by Europeans rather than with native foods that still exist in abundance.

Mutton stew was probably imported into the pueblos in the Santa Fe area from the Navajos, who live farther west. The Navajos were sheepherders whose sheep were originally from Mexico by way of Spain. The origin of fried bread, the bread that puffs up when it is fried in oil (lard is preferred) seems to be Navajo as well. Interestingly, a smaller version of this bread, called sopaipillas, is served in Santa Fe and Albuquerque restaurants. Wheat was imported by the Europeans; few Indians today cook with acorn flour. One traditional bread that probably antedates

Indeed they were. In fact, the introduction of livestock was so successful that the animals thrived even when they escaped into the wild. Within a century after the arrival of Columbus, the estimated New World population of cattle was 800,000, and of sheep, an astonishing 4.6 million. Sheep were introduced in 1598 by Capitán General Juan de Oñate. By the 1880s, there were millions of sheep in New Mexico and about 500,000 a year were exported. Today, the number of sheep produced remains at about half a million. With all that additional meat available, no wonder the cuisines of the Americas changed radically. Beef was readily added to such dishes as enchiladas, while pork was a favorite for *carne adovada*, the baked, chile-marinated dish. Domestic fowl such as chickens added diversity as their meat was incorporated into the corn cuisine of Santa Fe.

Wheat was also instrumental in changing the ways the Native Americans cooked by offering an alternative to corn for making the most basic food of all: bread. It was planted in such abundance throughout Mexico that by the middle of the sixteenth century, it was more common in the New World than in Spain, where wheat supplies had dropped and the people were eating rye bread. In New Mexico, wheat tortillas eventually became as popular as those made with corn.

It is not generally known that New Mexico and El Paso are the two oldest wine-producing regions in the United States. A Franciscan friar, Augustín Rodríguez, is credited with bringing grape vines to southern New Mexico in 1580, about a hundred years before the friars in California planted their vineyards. By 1662, priests of the Mesilla Valley in southern New Mexico were regularly producing sacramental wine for Mass.

It should be remembered that most of the Hispanic population of Santa Fe is the result of the early Spanish immigration from Mexico, and not from later Mexican immigration. The descendants of the early settlers have lived and prospered in the region for about four hundred years, and today, together with all other Hispanics, make up approximately 40 percent of the population. Thus the Hispanics of New Mexico refer to their Spanish heritage.

Hot, Hotter, Hottest

Surprisingly, the now ubiquitous chile peppers are not native to New Mexico at all, but were introduced from Central America by Spanish conquistadors in the sixteenth century. According to one member of the Antonio Espejo expedition of 1582–83, Baltasar Obregón, "They have no chile, but the natives were given some seed to plant." Even by 1601, chiles were still not on the list of Indian crops, according to colonist Francisco de Valverde, who also complained that mice were a pest that ate chile pods off the plants in the field.

After the Spanish began settlement of the area, the cultivation of chile peppers developed rapidly and soon they were grown all over New Mexico. It is likely that many different varieties were cultivated, including early forms of

jalapeños, serranos, anchos and pasillas. But one variety that adapted particularly well to New Mexico was a long green chile that turned red in the fall. Formerly called Anaheim because of its transfer to California around 1900, the New Mexican chiles were cultivated for hundreds of years in the region with such dedication that several distinct varieties developed. These varieties, Chimayó and Española, are still planted today in the fields they were grown in centuries ago; they are a small, distinct part of the tons of chile pods produced each year in New Mexico.

In 1846, William Emory, Chief Engineer of the Army's Topographic Unit, was surveying the New Mexico landscape and its customs. He described a meal eaten in Bernalillo, just north of Albuquerque: "Roast chicken, stuffed with onions; then mutton, boiled with onions; then followed by various other dishes, all dressed with the everlasting onion; and the whole terminated by chile, the glory of New Mexico."

Above: Las Cruces in southern New Mexico is well known for its bountiful chile harvest.

Emory went on to relate his experience with chiles: "Chile the Mexicans consider the chef-d'oeuvre of the cuisine, and seem really to revel in it; but the first mouthful brought the tears trickling down my cheeks, very much to the amusement of the spectators with their leather-lined throats. It was red pepper, stuffed with minced meat."

The earliest cultivated chiles in New Mexico were smaller than today's; indeed, they were (and still are, in some cases) considered a spice. But as the varieties developed and the size of the pods grew, the food value of chiles became evident. There was just one problem—the many sizes and shapes of the chile peppers made it very difficult for farmers to determine which chile they were growing from year to year. And there was no way to tell how large or how hot the pods might be until modern horticultural techniques produced more standardized chiles.

Today, New Mexico is by far the largest commercial producer of chile peppers in the United States, with about 35,000 acres under cultivation. All the primary dishes in New Mexican cuisine contain chile peppers: sauces, stews, *carne adovada*, enchiladas, tamales and many vegetable dishes. The intense use of chiles as a food rather than just as a spice or condiment is what differentiates New Mexican cuisine from that of Texas or Arizona. In neighboring states chile powders are used as a seasoning for beef broth or chicken broth–based "chili gravies," which are thickened with flour or cornstarch before being added to, say, enchiladas. In New Mexico the sauces are made from pure chiles and are thickened by reducing the crushed or puréed pods. New Mexico chile sauces are cooked and puréed, while salsas use fresh, uncooked ingredients. Debates rage over whether tomatoes should be used in cooked sauces such as red chile sauce, but traditional cooked red sauces do not contain tomatoes, though uncooked salsas do.

Chile peppers have become the de facto state symbol. Houses are adorned with strings of dried red chiles, called ristras. Images of the pods are emblazoned on signs, T-shirts, coffee mugs, hats and even underwear. In the late summer and early fall, the rich aroma of roasting chiles fills the air all over the state. "*A la primera cocinera se le va un chile entero*," goes one old Spanish *dicho* (saying): "To the best lady cook goes the whole chile." And the chile pepper is the single most important food in New Mexican cuisine.

The Arrival of the Anglos

Following Mexico's independence in 1821 and the opening of the Santa Fe Trail from Missouri, Santa Fe saw more and more trading (which had been prohibited by Spain, necessitating smuggling), and soon it was the terminus of two major trade routes from the east and the south. After Santa Fe fell to the Americans in 1846, the area really opened up as goods flooded in from the east.

Imported grains such as wheat became readily available with the arrival of the railroads. These grains were grown mostly on the eastern plains. However, imported flour was available and corn was raised in small plots by both Hispanics and Native Americans. Agriculture was so primitive in the region that one critic, Antonio Barreiro, wrote in 1832: "Agriculture is utterly neglected, for the inhabitants of this country do not sow any amount, as they might do to great profit without any doubt. They sow barely what they consider necessary for their maintenance for part of the year and the rest of the year they are exposed to a thousand miseries."

One such misery was described by Susan Magoffin, the teenaged bride of American trader and agent Samuel Magoffin. In her diary she describes her first taste of New Mexican green chile stew in 1846: "Oh how my heart sickened to say nothing of my stomach . . . [from] a mixture of meat, chilly verde & onions boiled together completing course No. 1. . . . There were a few mouthfuls taken, for I could not eat a dish so strong and unaccustomed to my palate." However, she did become accustomed to spicy food and even wrote a "cookery book" so that her friends in the States (New Mexico was still a territory, of course) could experience New Mexican cuisine.

By 1846, champagne and oysters were available, and flour for making bread sold for $2.50 per fanega. If that sounds expensive, knowing that a fanega was 144 pounds. About this time, a Lieutenant James Abert was traveling extensively throughout New Mexico. Later, in his book *Through the Country of the Comanche Indians*, he described the market at Santa Fe: "The markets have . . . great quantities of 'Chile Colorado' and 'verde,' 'cebollas' or onions, 'sandias' or watermelons, 'huevos' or eggs, 'uvas' or grapes, and 'pinones,' nuts of the pine tree."

Prices were relatively high. Corn was two dollars a bushel, beef and mutton eight to ten cents a pound, sugar and coffee were twenty-five cents a pound, and tea was very expensive at $1.25 a pound. About this time, W. W. H. Davis traveled to Santa Fe and sampled the native cuisine. In his book, *El Gringo*, he described his encounter: "The meal was a true Mexican dinner, and a fair sample of the style of living among the better class of people. The advance guard in the course of the dishes was boiled mutton and beans, the meat being young and tender, and well flavored. These were followed by a *sui generis* soup, different from any thing of the kind it had been my fortune to meet with before. It was filled with floating balls about the size of a musket bullet, which appeared to be a compound of flour and meat. Next came mutton stewed in chile (red peppers), the dressing of which was about the color of blood and almost as hot as so much molten lead."

After mentioning the *albóndigas* soup and the mutton, Davis described the standard beans, tortillas and *atole* (a corn drink) and then commented on chile: "Besides those already enumerated, there are other dishes, some of which have come down from the ancient inhabitants of the country. The chile they use in various ways—green, or verde, and in its dried state, the former being made into a sort of salad and is esteemed to be a great luxury."

The agricultural situation improved shortly after the U.S. Army raised its flag over Santa Fe's Palace of the Governors and New Mexico was opened up to further settlement by American pioneers. The introduction of modern tools and techniques and new crops such as apples, peas and melons helped the farmers greatly. By 1900, more than 5 million acres were under cultivation in New Mexico.

Santa Fe survived the Civil War without a scratch and did well under American control. Hotels and restaurants flourished with the coming of the railroad. Gradually, wheat crops surpassed corn crops in the state. However, wheat tortillas have not supplanted those made of corn; both are still equally popular.

Cattle had been introduced by Juan de Oñate but only assumed a significant role in New Mexico after the Civil War. By 1890, after the great cattle drives to the New Mexico gold mines to feed the miners, there were 1.34 million head of cattle in the state. Remarkably, the figure nearly a hundred years later (1988) was almost identical: 1.32 million head.

After the Homestead Act of 1862 and the arrival of the railroad between 1879 and 1882, settlers from the eastern United States flooded into the state. With the advent of the railroad came the first railroad restaurants, the Harvey House chain. New Mexico boasted sixteen of these establishments, including five that were the grandest of the system: Montezuma and Castañeda in Las Vegas, La Fonda in Santa Fe, Alvarado in Albuquerque and El Navajo in Gallup. Harvey hired young women between the ages of eighteen and thirty to be his hostesses and they were quite an attraction on the Western frontier, where women were

scarce. The humorist Will Rogers once said, "Fred Harvey kept the West in food and wives."

The Harvey Houses attempted to bring "civilized" food to the frontier, and early menus reveal dishes like chicken croquettes, baron of beef, turkey stuffed with oysters, vermicelli with cheese à la Italian, and the ever delectable calf's brains scrambled with ranch eggs. "Mexican" food was considered too "native" for travelers and rarely appeared on upscale hotel and restaurant menus.

The railroads brought the settlers and these pioneers brought new food crops. At first, vegetables such as tomatoes, asparagus, cabbage, carrots, lettuce, onions and peas were produced in home gardens on a small scale, but when extensive irrigation facilities were constructed in the early twentieth century, commercial vegetable production began.

During the years following World War I, Santa Fe began to emerge from obscurity as the city—and the rest of the state—was discovered by artists such as Peter Hurd and Georgia O'Keeffe, authors such as Willa Cather and D. H. Lawrence, and other prominent sculptors, poets, photographers and musicians. The high concentration of artists in the city, combined with Santa Fe's tradition as an Indian trading center, produced one of the top art markets in the world. More than 150 galleries (concentrated around the Plaza and along Canyon Road) now feature local as well as international artists, and special events such as Indian Market in mid-August ensure that the ancient artistic traditions are kept alive.

In the decades after World War I, the cuisines of Santa Fe, however, remained fairly segregated: an Indian-Hispanic hybrid cuisine served in the pueblos; hotels offered mostly standard meat and potatoes eastern-style; and the traditional New Mexican chile-based cuisine was served in Hispanic houses and restaurants. But major culinary changes would occur as Santa Fe became one of the top ten tourist destinations in the country.

OPPOSITE: Capsaicinoids, the heat-producing substances in chile peppers, can be seen here as golden droplets in the center below the seeds. ABOVE: Wagon trains bringing goods from the eastern states, as well as luxuries from Europe, began making regular trips across the plains from Missouri in the 1820s. The momentous opening of the Sante Fe Trail is reenacted each year.

Celebrations and Festivals

Santa Feans love to party, and the entire year seems to revolve around the many fiestas—one after another. Even calling these celebrations "markets" doesn't prevent people from partying.

Spanish Market, held during the last weekend in July for more than forty-five years, showcases the arts and crafts of New Mexico's Hispanic artisans. There is the Traditional Spanish Market, held on the Plaza, and the Contemporary Spanish Market, held in the courtyard of the Palace of the Governors. The crafts sold include santos (carved wooden saints), tinwork, embroidery, jewelry, weaving and hand-made furniture

Indian Market, held around the Plaza during a weekend in mid-August for more than seventy-five years, is probably the finest single show of Indian arts and crafts in the United States. Collectors travel from all over the world to this event, which features only Indian-made arts and crafts. As with Spanish Market, numerous food booths featuring the local street fare of tacos, tostadas and burritos are also set up.

The Santa Fe Wine and Chile Festival is held in mid-September, and the events take place in various restaurants and cooking schools. A grand tasting is held in a tent in the parking lot of a downtown hotel and features traditional and innovative food prepared by Santa Fe's best restaurants, and wines from New Mexico, Texas and California wineries.

One of the largest celebrations in Santa Fe is Fiesta de Santa Fe, which was established in 1712 by Don Diego de Vargas to commemorate the reoccupation of New Mexico by the Spanish. It begins the Friday after Labor Day in Fort Marcy Park with the burning of Zozobra, a forty-foot-tall effigy representing Old Man Gloom. Afterward, the party moves to the Plaza and downtown area for two more days of parades, dancing, singing, religious processions, and booths filled with arts, crafts and traditional food. The best time to visit is during a feast day, for you can be sure that a ceremony or dance will take place. Of special fun are the grab or throw days. Many Native Americans are named for Catholic saints and on each saint's day, all pueblo members with that name go up on the roof and throw something down to the crowd that travels from house to house. Sweets such as commercial candy, apples, prizes, or even small plastic trash cans are among the items that get thrown. Historically, water would be flung from gourds to encourage rain and although it is still done, children seem to prefer water balloons to gourds! You may get wet, but you'll have a good time.

During the feast days at the Indian pueblos, tourists are welcome during most of the ceremonies and dances and may even be invited to join in. However, there is a definite etiquette to be observed. Enter a home by invitation only, and if invited to eat (which is common) don't refuse and

don't linger, as others will be invited to take your place. Limit your questions—asking too many will be viewed as inconsiderate. And don't walk across the plaza or dance area, look into kivas or talk to dancers during the ceremonies; remember that these are religious shrines and activities.

It is always best to check with the tribal or tourist office before wandering into a pueblo. They can steer you to craftspeople and places of interest and inform you of the particular rules governing that pueblo. Always respect Indian traditions when you're on their land; it is a sovereign nation, and you are subject to their laws and regulations.

Other special events in Santa Fe include Rodeo de Santa Fe, which began in the 1940s and has steadily grown into a popular regional competition. It happens in early July, and between three and five hundred cowboys compete in riding, roping and racing events. The Santa Fe Festival of the Arts is held in October, and history buffs will enjoy the Mountain Man Rendezvous and Buffalo Roast held in mid-August on the Plaza.

The Christmas season in New Mexico always brings its distinctive sights, aromas and tastes. The traditional colors of the season are evident in the red and green New Mexican chiles; the aroma of burning piñon pine permeates the air. The Spanish brought Christmas to the Southwest about four hundred years ago, but the Pueblo Indians were already celebrating this time of the year with a number of feast days. After the harvest was stored for the winter, dances were performed both to give thanks for the bounty and to apologize for the necessity of having to hunt for winter food. These traditions continue to this day.

Probably no other image symbolizes the Christmas season in New Mexico more than the luminarias that line walkways and outline buildings and houses throughout the state. Originally, little crisscross fires of piñon wood were lit on Christmas Eve to light the Christ child's way. With the advent of the square-bottomed brown paper bag, the bonfires were replaced with a votive candle anchored in sand in the bag—and the farolito (little lantern) was born. Whether called luminarias or farolitos, they are traditionally lit only on December 24, *la noche buena*; and with most electric lights turned off, they weave a quiet, soft spell.

Many of the tastes of the season are prepared from recipes handed down from generation to generation. These recipes incorporate a mixture of cultures—Indian, Spanish and Anglo—and utilize locally available foodstuffs, including corn for flour or dried for use in stews, whole pods of chile from the strings of ristras and meat from live-stock that could not be kept over the winter. Stews like posole were kept on the stove to feed friends stopping by after Mass or for hosting neighborhood posadas, Spanish plays enacting Mary and Joseph's search for an inn. Many of these traditions continue today in New Mexico homes. For example, it is not unusual for spectators attending Indian dances at a pueblo on Christmas Eve to be invited into a home for tamales, a bowl of posole or green chile stew, or even some *carne adovada*. Dessert would be flan (custard), natillas (soft custard) or *biscochitos* (anise-flavored shortbread cookies). It would be impolite to refuse the invitation to dine, since it is a part of the New Mexican Christmas tradition for everyone who stops by.

Dining Out in Santa Fe

Within just a few blocks of the Plaza in Santa Fe, foodies can indulge every gastronomic whim imaginable. Want to buy the hottest salsa known to man? Like some to-die-for blue corn enchiladas with delicious red chile? Care to taste some New Mexican wines and beers? Need a ristra for your front porch? It's all here in Santa Fe.

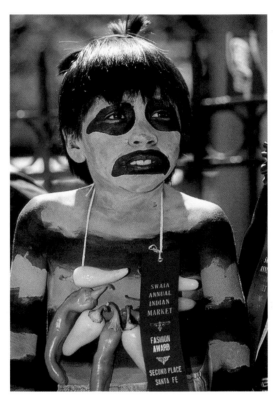

There are probably more fine restaurants per capita in Santa Fe than anywhere else in the United States and this is undoubtedly the result of tourism.

As is true of New Mexico in general, people living in and visiting the City Different love their food spicy hot. In fact, a study done a few years ago determined that Santa Fe is the fiery food capital of the country. Despite the spiciness of the Santa Fe food, visitors should note that there is a wide variety of cuisines available to sample because Santa Fe attracts great culinary artists as well as great visual artists. There isn't space here to mention all of the city's great restaurants, so we have described only our personal favorites.

Travel back in time as you reach the end of the Santa Fe Trail at **La Fonda** hotel and restaurant (100 E. San Francisco Street), a mainstay in Santa Fe for three hundred years. Although the current structure is only eighty years old, it is filled with the charm of Old Santa Fe and features thick adobe walls, high ceilings, carved wood furniture, stone floors and big inviting fireplaces. The restaurant is in an atrium with painted windows and turn-of-the-century art, including works by legendary American artist Georgia O'Keeffe.

The menu is inspired by the cuisines of Old Mexico and Spain and contains items such as Grilled Quail Breast with Ancho Chile Glaze served in a Sweet Potato Taco, Wild Boar Carnitas and rattlesnake dishes.

From artists to outlaws, much of Santa Fe's colorful history has been witnessed at the bar of **El Farol** (808 Canyon Road), a popular social spot for locals since 1835. The stories say that it was the scene of many gunfights, and in the 1950s, famed artist Alfred Morang paid his tab by painting a mural on one of the walls. Hidden underneath paneling for a number of years, his work has now been restored and continues to be a popular attraction. The fare is traditional Spanish and the specialties are tapas (they even have a designated Tapas Room), paella and Spanish wines.

The tradition of great restaurants in Santa Fe during the modern era was born more than forty-five years ago when Rosalea Murphy opened **The Pink Adobe** (406 Old Santa Fe Trail). As Rosalea recalls, when "the Pink" first opened, Santa Fe was not the tourist mecca it is today, but rather a "lazy, sleepy town." She served twenty-five-cent "Pink Dobeburgers," then imported chicken enchiladas from Mexico, and eventually became the first chef in Santa Fe to serve seafood. Today, the restaurant is located in a former barracks for Spanish soldiers, Barrio de Analco, one of the oldest parts of Santa Fe. Despite its name, the Pink Adobe is no longer pink but rather a shade of sand-stone. Santa Fe's Historical Design Review Board has refused to allow the restaurant to be painted its original color because, according to the board, pink is not an earth tone. During a hearing on the issue, Rosalea presented several samples of pink rocks collected in the desert and mountains around Santa Fe, but the board still refused.

The **Coyote Cafe** (132 West Water Street) offers a truly unique dining experience because anthropologist-turned-chef Mark Miller presents a different menu each day, recreating Southwestern and Latin American dishes that predate the arrival of Europeans. It is difficult to suggest any one particular menu item because they change so much, but some past menus have included Barbecued

Duck Crepas, layered corn crepes with roast duck, barbecue sauce, and corn chile relish; and Red Chile Quail, fresh Texas bobwhite quail marinated in dried chiles and wild mushrooms.

"My café is small but lively," says Katharine Kagel, chef-owner of **Cafe Pasqual**'s (121 Don Gaspar Avenue), which has been in business since 1979. Located one block from the historic Plaza, the café serves the food of New and Old Mexico, as well as New American Cuisine. During the day, the atmosphere is informal, but the mood changes at dinnertime when the white tablecloths come out and the wine service begins. Signature dishes include Huevos Motuleños, a Yucatán egg dish, and Chicken Mole Presciliano, a Pueblo-style family recipe made with twenty different ingredients. The café also boasts an art gallery that features Mexican murals, traditional Apache cookware and jewelry.

The three cultures of Santa Fe come together in the food and the architecture of **Inn of the Anasazi** (113 Washington Avenue), where Native American spirituality, Mexican flair and European practicality define the experience. Diners can settle in on cozy bancos to warm their bones by the fire and their insides with cutting-edge dishes like Grilled Tortilla and Lime Soup with Barbecued Yellow Tomato Salsa and Cilantro Corn Oil, a popular appetizer that has been on the menu since the award-winning restaurant opened in 1991.

La Casa Sena (125 East Palace Avenue) was expanded from a small house to a thirty-three-room adobe hacienda in 1868 by a prominent Santa Fe family. The courtyard is now one of the city's most beautiful outdoor dining spots. The restaurant opened in 1983 and serves innovative dishes such as Grilled Pepita Crusted Salmon with Ancho Chile Hollandaise and Goat Cheese Epazote Quesadilla.

Serving traditional northern New Mexico cuisine, **Maria's New Mexican Kitchen** (555 West Cordova Road) was originally a take-out place started in the early 1950s by Maria, the wife of a local politician. After several years she sold it, and it has grown since. Owner Al Lucero says that his place was the first to introduce fajitas to Santa Fe back in 1985. However, margaritas, over seventy-five of them, are Maria's main claim to fame. They are made with only the best authentic tequilas and are hand-shaken never stirred.

The **Santacafé** (231 Washington Street), a "Southwest American Bistro" in a 150-year-old building, has been open since 1983 and is a local favorite for its innovative menu and celebrity-watching opportunities. Its decor is not traditional Southwestern but stark minimalist, with bare off-white walls. The signature dish is Crispy Calamari with Lime Dipping Sauce, and the menu includes Grilled Rack of Lamb with Pasilla Chile Sauce and Roasted Corn-shiitake Mushroom Salsa. It has been named a top-rated restaurant by Zagat's guide.

Since 1989, the **Santa Fe School of Cooking** (116 West San Francisco Street) has defined traditional New Mexican cooking and has set the tone for contemporary Southwest cuisine with dishes like Lime-Marinated Grilled Salmon with Ginger-lime Butter. "We mirror Santa Fe," says Susan Curtis, founder of the school. Many Santa Fe chefs have taught or studied here and instruction is open to all.

Paul's Restaurant of Santa Fe (72 West Marcy Street) is an intimate place that incorporates the best of all worlds, from its folksy yet modern atmosphere to its eclectic cuisine. "We don't follow trends," says Paul Hunsicker, who opened the restaurant in 1990. His menu combines flavors from around the world in dishes like Baked Salmon in a Pecan Herb Crust and Red Chile Duck Wontons.

The many innovations of the new Southwestern chefs, while surprising, are fully in keeping with the past. In New Mexico, the traditional cuisine based on corn, beans, squash and chiles will probably be cooked for centuries to come. But this doesn't mean that it has to be static. And today's chefs are creating exciting new food by blending the ideas of other cultures with the fundamentals of Southwestern cookery and ingredients in wonderful new ways.

The Santa Fe Kitchen

A guide to essential utensils, cooking methods and ingredients

Despite the food of Santa Fe seeming to be quite exotic, the equipment necessary to cook it is not strange at all. The traditional utensils, originally from Mexico, are all but obsolete in these days of premade tortillas and electrical appliances. In earlier times, a *metlapil*, a cylindrical stone, would be rolled on a **metate**, a flat, rectangular stone, to grind the corn kernels for tortillas. After the corn was ground and a masa (corn dough) made, corn tortillas would be prepared with a rolling pin, but the Spanish developed the first wooden **tortilla presses** to make the process easier. Presses were hand carved from mesquite or made of metal. Now more commonly made of cast aluminum or iron, a press consists of two plates, a hinge and a handle that you press to flatten and shape the ball of masa. Wheat tortillas have always been prepared with a rolling pin and fingertips. After flattening, the tortillas would be cooked on a **comal** (griddle).

A *molcajete y tejolote*—a volcanic-rock mortar and pestle—would be used to grind spices or to make salsas for tortilla dishes. A *molinillo*, a short stick with indentations in the bulb at its tip, was used (and still is), to prepare frothy hot chocolate.

In the modern Santa Fe kitchen, a food processor or blender has taken over the tasks of the metates and *molcajetes* and a comal has been replaced by a **griddle** or **cast-iron skillet**. Casseroles have replaced *cazuelas*, the glazed earthenware pots ubiquitious in Southwestern antique shops.

A **spice mill** is handy to have not only for grinding spices but for grinding chiles into powder. When you grind chiles, you may want to wear a paint mask to avoid breathing in the powder. You will need air-tight containers to store ground chile powders.

For making chile sauce, an eight-quart **Dutch oven** is recommended. A **steamer** is useful for cooking tamales. A **charcoal** or **gas grill** is useful for roasting chiles and to grill meat, although chiles can be roasted in a conventional oven or toaster oven as well. A **deep fryer** is ideal for making sopaipillas, the puffed-up bread. A heavy saucepan can be substituted if you do not have a deep fryer.

Making Corn Tortillas

Tlaxcallim (corn tortillas) were the principal food of both the Mayas and the Aztecs as early as 10,000 b.c. Both cultures worshiped corn and the Mayas believed that humans were created from corn dough (masa). Corn tortillas are made in much the same way today as they have been for centuries. Dried corn kernels are briefly cooked in a solution of water and unslaked lime (calcium hydroxide), or "builder's lime," to remove their tough skin and soften them enough to grind. The resulting *nixtamal* is combined with water to form masa.

Tortillas can only be made from masa; cornmeal will not work. If you cannot purchase ready-to-use masa, masa harina, which is dehydrated *nixtamal*, is available in many grocery stores alongside the flour or from a number of mail-order sources.

There are a variety of ways to form corn tortillas. The most difficult method is by hand. A flattened ball of masa about 1 in ($2^1/_2$ cm) in diameter is worked between the hands in a rapid, smooth motion. Mastering this art is not as easy as it looks and takes a lot of practice!

To use a tortilla press, make the dough using the recipe on page 97. Once your masa balls are ready, cover the bottom plate of the press with a piece of heavy plastic wrap or wax paper that is a little larger than the press. Place the ball on the press a little off center, toward the hinge. Cover the dough with another piece of plastic, close the press and push the handle down hard. Open the press, peel off the top piece of plastic, place the tortilla plastic side up on one hand, remove the remaining plastic, and gently roll the tortilla onto a heated comal or skillet to cook. Don't try to peel the tortilla off the plastic—trust us, it won't work.

If you don't have a press, you can roll out the masa between two pieces of plastic wrap with a rolling pin. Remove the plastic as described above.

Making Flour Tortillas

The Spanish name tortilla comes from the word *torta*, which means "round cake," an apt description of this flat, unleavened bread. When the Spanish brought wheat to the Western Hemisphere, the flour tortilla (*tortilla de harina*) was born.

Flour tortillas are popular in the northern states of Mexico and in the southwestern United States, and they vary in size and thickness. Those made in California and Arizona are much thinner than those made in New Mexico. Unlike corn tortillas, flour tortillas contain fat. Lard is traditionally used, which tends to result in a crumbly tortilla, but those made with vegetable shortening can sometimes be bland. A combination of both produces a good tortilla.

Flour tortillas aren't formed by hand or in a press—they must be rolled because of the gluten in the wheat. A small rolling pin is best because it applies less pressure and results in a lighter tortilla. The best and least expensive rolling pin and the one most often found in Mexico, is simply a length of broom handle. You can also use a wooden

Making Corn Tortillas

Step 1: Cover the bottom plate with plastic wrap, position the ball of masa and cover it with another sheet of wrap.

Step 2: Lower the handle of the press and apply firm pressure.

Step 3: Open the press, lift off the top plastic, pick up the tortilla and place it on your palm, plastic side up. Peel away the remaining sheet of plastic.

Roasting Chiles

Step 1: Make a slit at the top of each chile for the steam to escape. Roast over an open flame, turning until the skin blisters on all sides.

Step 2: Wrap the blistered chiles in a damp cloth for a few minutes. The steam will loosen the skin.

Step 3: Gently peel the skin off. If you have sensitive skin you may want to wear gloves to do this.

Seeding and Soaking Dried Chiles

Step 1: Cut open the dried chiles lengthwise. If you plan to stuff them, make a slit and empty them through it.

Step 2: Remove the seeds and the tough, white membranes.

Step 3: Soak them in warm water only long enough to soften them, 15 to 20 minutes.

1. piñon nuts 2. lentils 3. epazote
4. mexican oregano 5. *atole*
6. canela (cinnamon) 7. *piloncillo*
(brown sugar) 8. posole
9. *manzanilla* (camomile)
10. crushed chiles 11. red chile
powder 12. pinto beans 13. chicos
14. coriander seeds 15. green
chile powder 16. black beans
17. blue corn 18. anasazi beans

dowel from the hardware store. Whichever you choose, be sure to wash it well before you use it.

You don't roll a tortilla as you do a pie crust. Instead, lightly flour a smooth surface and using your fingers, pinch out pieces of dough about 1 1/2 in (4 cm) in diameter. Then, flatten each piece of dough and form it into a circle. With the rolling pin, roll a circle of dough front and back and then rotate it a quarter turn. Flip the tortilla over every few rotations and roll it until it is very round and thin. Once you have completed this first step, drape the tortilla over one hand and gradually stretch the dough out from around the edges with the other. This too takes practice. The finished tortilla should be 7 in (18 cm) or 8 in (20 cm) in diameter.

Fry the raw tortilla in a heated comal or skillet with a little oil until it is firm, turning it only once. If it puffs up, flatten it with a spatula.

Although the best tortillas are fresh and warm, you can store them in the refrigerator for up to a week or freeze them. Cold tortillas need to be warmed in order to soften them and there are a number of ways to do so. To steam them, put 1/2 in (1 cm) of water in a steamer and heat two tortillas at a time for 1 minute—no longer, or they will become soft and soggy—and then let them stand for 15 minutes. You can also cover a stack of tortillas with foil and heat them for 15 minutes in a 325°F oven. For faster results, wrap them in a towel and microwave them for 20 to 30 seconds on full power. If you have a gas stove, the quickest and easiest way is to heat them for a couple of seconds on each side over an open burner.

Preparing Chile Peppers

Travelers to New Mexico in the late summer and early fall are treated to the sight of forty-pound sacks of potent green chiles at roadside stands and are often tempted to buy one. But then what do you do with them?

New Mexican chiles are usually blistered and peeled before being ground or cooked. Blistering the chile is the process of roasting the fresh pods to the point at which the tough transparent skin separates from the meat of the chile so it can be removed. This roasting is what gives New Mexican chile sauces their distinctive burnt, smoky flavor. Fresh, firm chiles are the easiest to peel. As chiles age, the flesh becomes soft and the skin starts to wrinkle and tends to fall apart during processing. Should you have to use one with a slightly wrinkled skin, rub it with a little vegetable oil before blistering.

To roast and peel chiles, first cut a small slit close to the stem end so that the steam can escape and the pod won't explode. The chiles can be placed on a baking sheet and put directly under the broiler, or on a screen on the stovetop. They can also be plunged into hot cooking oil to loosen the skin.

Our favorite method, which involves meditation with a six-pack of Santa Fe Pale Ale, is to place the pods on a charcoal grill about 5 in (13 cm) or 6 in (15 cm) from the coals. Blisters will soon indicate that the skin is separating;

be sure to turn them as they cook so that the chiles are blistered all over, or they will not peel properly. Although the chiles may burn slightly, take care that they do not blacken (they will be nearly impossible to peel).

Immediately wrap the chiles in damp paper towels and place them in a plastic bag to steam for 10 to 15 minutes. The best way to avoid chile burns from the capsaicin that gives chiles their heat is to wear rubber gloves during the peeling process. Remove the skin, stem and seeds of each pod and chop the flesh coarsely. Place the chopped chile in plastic ice cube trays and freeze it solid. Pop out the cubes and place them in Ziploc freezer bags: you'll have an easy access to whatever amount of chile that is needed for a recipe. The taste of Santa Fe will keep in your freezer for at least a year.

Dried chile pods should be stored in airtight containers to prevent insect damage, but of course many people buy the long strings, or ristras, of red chiles and simply pluck them off as needed. But ristras are designed for dry climates and suffer in excess humidity. The best storage for dried pods is in self-sealing plastic bags in the freezer. Some sauces require that you remove the seeds and membranes of dried chiles and soak them in warm water before using them.

Grinding chiles into powders is an efficient way to store them in small spaces, but be sure to keep them in airtight containers away from sunlight, to prevent oxidation and fading. To make chile powder, the pods must be thoroughly dried until they are brittle. Use a microwave on low power or a 200°F oven for a few hours. The next step is to grind the chiles into powder. Be sure to wear a paint mask for at least some protection against inhaling the pungent capsaicin fumes. Using a spice mill or coffee grinder, grind the chiles to the desired consistency. They may be ground to a fine powder called *molido* or be coarsely ground with some of the seeds, which is called *quebrado*.

A Guide to Chiles

poblano New Mexican (green) New Mexican (red) pasilla ancho

There are so many different kinds of chiles that it can be hard to keep them straight. But the differences in flavor are so significant, that it's worth trying to learn to identify the important ones. The principal chile peppers in Santa Fe cooking are the New Mexican varieties, called **Anaheims** in California. More than 35,000 acres are under cultivation in New Mexico. In their fresh form, they are called simply **green chiles**, and the pods are roasted and peeled before use. Fresh red pods can also be used in this manner. When dried, red chiles can be used whole or ground into powder. At flea markets in Santa Fe and Albuquerque you will find stands where farmers sell their own red and green chile powders, ground chipotle and ristras of every size.

There are a number of varieties of New Mexican chiles and all are readily available in Santa Fe. They range from the relatively mild **Big Jim**, **NuMex Joe E. Parker** and **No. 6-4** that are grown in the southern part of the state to the hotter northern varieties such as **Barker**, **Española** and **Velarde**. Incidentally, **Hatch** chile is not a variety but merely a geographical designation of the chile-growing region around Hatch, in the Rio Grande Valley of southern New Mexico. In addition to the New Mexican varieties, many Mexican chiles appear in northern New Mexican cooking. They are easily obtained in markets, shops and natural-food supermarkets. Each chile has an entirely different flavor profile, so don't substitute randomly. Appropriate substitutions are suggested.

The **ancho** is the dried form of the **poblano**. The fresh

green pods range in length from 3 to 6 in (8 to 15 cm) and in width from 3 to 4 in (8 to 10 cm). The fresh pods are roasted and peeled; then they are stuffed with meat, vegetables or cheese to make *chiles rellenos*, cut into strips, chopped, or sometimes ground into a powder. The reddish-brown anchos are usually toasted on a griddle and rehydrated before they are used. The anchos have a flavor that is often described as tasting like raisins. This variety is rather mild. Pasilla chiles may be substituted for anchos.

The spherical **cascabel** chile is about $1^{1}/_{2}$ in (4 cm) in diameter and is most frequently used in its dried form. When the chile is dry, the seeds rattle in the pod—accounting for its name, which translates roughly as "jingle bell." Cascabels are used in sauces and to spice up many other dishes, such as soups and stews. Cascabels have medium heat. Substitute guajillo chiles if you can't find cascabels.

Literally, a **chipotle** is any smoked chile, but the term generally refers to a jalapeño that has been partially dried in the sun and then smoked. Dark brown or red, about 2 in (5 cm) long and 1 in ($2^{1}/_{2}$ cm) wide, they come in two forms: dried, or canned in an adobo sauce, which is a tomato-based sauce. Dried chipotles are rehydrated before use and are sometimes ground into powder. These chiles are moderately hot and have a wonderfully complex flavor. There is no real substitute for these smoked chiles.

The name **de Árbol** means "tree chile," an allusion to the appearance of the plant. About 3 in (8 cm) long and

cayenne japonés habanero

serrano　　　　　jalapeño　　　　　yellow hot　　　　　chipotle　　　　　de Árbol

$^3/_8$ in (1 cm) wide, these medium hot dried pods are used in cooked sauces of all kinds and are sometimes ground into a powder. A good substitute is mirasol.

Similar in appearance to New Mexican varieties, **guajillos** are used mostly in their dry form. They are 4 to 6 in (10 to 15 cm) long and about $1^1/_2$ in (4 cm) wide. The pods are orange-red, medium hot and are used primarily in sauces. The substitute is dried red New Mexican chiles.

Grown in the Yucatán Peninsula, the lantern-shaped, orange **habanero** chiles are the hottest peppers in the world. The pods are about $1^1/_2$ in (4 cm) long and 1 in ($2^1/_2$ cm) wide and have a distinctive aroma that is fruity and apricot-like. They are used in their fresh form in Mexico but also appear dried in the United States and Canada. The fresh pods are used extensively in salsas and other Yucatecan dishes. There is no substitute for the flavor of fresh habaneros; use the hottest fresh chiles you can find, such as cayenne or Thai. For dried habaneros, substitute piquín.

Perhaps the most common chile in Mexico, the familiar **jalapeño** is 1 to 2 in ($2^1/_2$ to 5 cm) long and about $^3/_4$ in (2 cm) wide. Unless they are smoked to create chipotles, jalapeños are used exclusively fresh in a great number of dishes. They have medium heat and are often found pickled in cans. To pickle them, they are sautéed with spices then covered with vinegar and stored in a dark place to develop the flavor. Serranos may be substituted.

The name **mirasol** means "looking at the sun," an allu-sion to the erect pods, which measure up to 4 in (10 cm) long and $^3/_4$ in (2 cm) wide. The medium-hot pods are used dried in sauces and meat dishes and are sometimes ground into powder. The substitute is de Árbol.

Fresh **pasilla** chiles are called **chilacas** and are used in a similar manner to New Mexican varieties or poblanos. When dried, the pods are 5 to 6 in (13 to 15 cm) long and about $1^1/_2$ in (4 cm) wide. They are used in sauces and may be stuffed. The pods are mild and are sometimes ground into powder. As the name "little raisin" implies, the pods have an aroma and flavor like raisin. The substitute for pasilla is ancho.

The small, erect **piquín** pods are less than 1 in ($2^1/_2$ cm) long and $^1/_2$ in (1 cm) wide; they usually resemble miniature bullets. **Chiltepíns** were the only chile that the Native Americans cultivated in the wild before the arrival of the Spanish. They are spherical piquíns that measure about $^1/_4$ in ($^1/_2$ cm) in diameter. Their name is believed to be derived from the Aztec words *chilli* and *tecpintl*, meaning "flea chile," an allusion to the chiltepín's sharp bite. The pods of both are used in salsas, soups and stews, or ground into powder. They are hot to extremely hot. The substitute is dried habanero.

Both the red and green varieties of the **serrano** chile are used fresh. Measuring 1 to 3 in ($2^1/_2$ to 8 cm) long and $^1/_2$ in (1 cm) wide, it is the chile of choice in Mexico for fresh salsas and has medium heat. The name means "mountain chile" or "highland chile." The serrano is often found pickled in cans. Jalapeño is a good substitute.

piquín　　　chiltepín　　　　　　　cascabel　　　　　　　morita

Authentic Santa Fe Ingredients

Achiote, the orange-colored seeds of the tropical annatto tree, is commonly used as a coloring agent and a seasoning. **Achiote paste** or annatto seed paste typically contains ground annatto seeds mixed with garlic, salt and spices. When diluted with a small amount of vinegar or citrus juice, it makes a wonderful marinade for beef, pork or poultry. Achiote paste can be found in Hispanic grocery stores.

Aniseed is the fruit of the anise plant and comes from the Middle East. It is one of the oldest spices and is also used medicinally. The spice contains essential oils and other ingredients which give it a strong licorice flavor. Aniseed is used to make bizcochitos, a type of cookie. It can be found in most well-stocked supermarkets. Substitute fennel seed, if necessary.

Arugula, also known as rocket, is a tasty green that has a flavor and texture that changes drastically over its lifespan. Young arugula leaves are soft and mild; more mature leaves are tougher and sharper, to the point of being peppery. When using arugula in salad, look for young, bright green leaves.

Beans are widely used in Santa Fe cuisine and most are varieties of kid-

ney beans, *Phaseolus vulgaris*. By far the most popular beans in New Mexico are **pinto beans,** but other varieties are slowly being adopted into Santa Fe cuisine. Pinto beans are so named because of their brown-and-white "painted" appearance. They are boiled with spices and chiles, and are often mashed and refried. The **black turtle beans** are small black beans commonly used in Caribbean soups or stews. Sometimes they are refried. The **white Aztec beans,** native to the Southwest, are large round white beans with a nutty flavor. The **New Mexican black appaloosa beans,** also native, are spotted black-and-white bush beans that are often used in place of pinto beans.

Bell Peppers, known as capsicums, have a crunchy texture and a fresh, tangy taste. The most popular peppers are greed and red, but sweeter yellow and orange peppers have become more widely available. In New Mexican cuisine, bell peppers make a colorful addition to soups and side dishes and are sautéed with onions for fajitas and quesadillas.

Cheese is an important ingredient in Santa Fe cuisine. The American cheeses used most commonly in

Santa Fe are Monterey jack, cheddar, and goat cheese. However, some Mexican cheeses are available, and the following are recommended. Adobera cheese, which is shaped like an adobe brick, looks and tastes like Monterey jack but holds its shape when heated. Asadero, which means "broiler" or "roaster" cheese is from Coahuila. This mild, soft, often braided cheese is sold in tortilla-sized slices or wound into balls. Chihuahua is a mild, spongy, creamy and pale yellow cheese that gets stringy when it is heated. It is also called *queso menonita*. Substitute feta cheese if you can't obtain it. Fresco is a fresh, salty, crumbly white cheese served with salads and salsas. Also called *queso blanco, ranchero, quesito*, and *estilo casero*. Substitute feta if you can't obtain it.

Chipotles en adobo are smoked red jalapeño that have been stewed in vinegar, tomato sauce and spices. They add warm heat and a distinctive smoky flavor to many recipes. Canned *chipotles en adobo* are available in many supermarkets, or you can easily make your own with the following recipe:

7 to 10 chipotle chiles, stemmed and
    split lengthwise
$1/2$ small onion, sliced
5 tablespoons cider vinegar
2 cloves garlic, sliced
4 tablespoons tomato ketchup
$1/4$ teaspoon salt
3 cups (750 ml) of water

Bring all the ingredients to a boil in a saucepan, then reduce the heat and simmer for about $1^1/_2$ hours, or until the chiles are tender and the sauce has reduced by one-third. Store in an airtight container in the refrigerator for up to 3 weeks. This makes about 1 cup (250 ml) of sauce.

Note: You can purée the chiles and the liquid in a food processor, strain to remove the seeds, and portion into an ice-cube tray to freeze for later use. Store the frozen cubes in a plastic bag in the freezer.

Chorizo is a spicy sausage made from ground pork, garlic and red chile powder. It is sometimes placed in casings but most often is served crumbly. Substitute Italian sausage or any spicy pork sausage.

Cilantro is an annual herb (*Coriandrum sativum*) with seeds that are known as coriander. The fresh leaves are commonly used in salsas and soups. Substitute Italian parsley, but the flavor is slightly different.

Corn is a popular ingredient in the Santa Fe kitchen. Three main types are used: yellow, white and blue. Multicolored Indian corn is mostly used for decoration. Blue corn is particularly popular for its slightly nutty taste. The following products can be made from any of the three main varieties: **Posole** is corn kernels that have been treated with lime to remove their tough skin; it is then used in the pork and chile stew called posole. **Chicos** are dried corn kernels that are steamed and added to soups and stews. No lime is used in the process. **Corn husks**, softened in hot water, are used as a wrapping for tamales. **Cornmeal** is the coarsely ground dried corn for making cornbread. **Cornflour** is the finely ground, lime-treated dried corn in the dough called masa.

Cumin, known as *comino* in Spanish, is an annual herb (*Cuminum cyminum*) whose seeds (used whole or powdered) have a distinctive, musty odor. It is used to flavor sauces and main dishes.

Epazote, known as "Ambrosia" in English, is a strong and bitter perennial herb (*Chenopodium ambrosioides*) used primarily to flavor beans because it is said to aid in their digestion. It can be used either fresh or dry.

Habanero sauce is made from crushed chiles cooked with tomatoes, onions, garlic, fruits, herbs and spices. Many varieties and styles of commercial habanero sauce are available in the supermarkets today. One of the best-known is Tabasco Habanero Sauce. If preferred, you can make your own habanero sauce by following the recipe below:

1 to 3 dried habanero peppers
1 cup (250 ml) water
$1/3$ cup (85 ml) red wine vinegar
1 tablespoon paprika
1 teaspoon cumin
1 teaspoon salt

Grind the habanero peppers in a mortar until fine, then combine it with all the other ingredients and bring to a boil in a saucepan. Simmer for about 10 minutes and remove from the heat. Purée the mixture in a blender until smooth and store in an airtight container in the refrigerator for up to several weeks. This makes about 1 cup (250 ml) of sauce.

Huitlacoche, also spelled Acuitlacoche, is a fungus that grows on corn and is used like mushrooms in New Mexico cooking. It is considered a delicacy that adds a unique, earthy flavor to quesadillas, tamales, crepes, soups and other dishes. Huitlacoche is cultivated in Mexico where it is available fresh, but most commonly available canned in Hispanic grocery stores.

Jicama, also known as the Mexican potato, is a white tuber (*Pachyrhizus erosus*) shaped like a large, flattened top that is used in salads. An import from Mexico, it tastes like a cross between an apple and a potato. It is crunchy and sweet, and can be eaten either raw or cooked.

Limes are used fresh in almost all types of New Mexican dishes; the juice is stirred in to sauces and salsas. They are squeezed over seafood to make ceviche, rubbed onto meats before grilling and splashed into margaritas. Their most important function, however, is extinguishing the fire of spicy dishes.

Masa is fresh dough made from corn that has been treated with lime and partially cooked. It is used to make tortillas and tamales. **Masa harina** literally means dough flour and is made from dried masa that is ground into a fine powder. Fresh masa can sometimes be found in Hispanic grocery stores. Masa harina is easier to find and is sometimes available at well-stocked supermarkets.

Mexican chocolate is chocolate with sugar and cinnamon that comes in pressed and scored cakes. It is used to make a frothy, rich hot chocolate and in baking.

Mexican cinnamon, also known as *canela*, refers to the softer loose-bark variety grown in Ceylon rather than the more commonly found hard-stick Cassia bark normally sold as cinnamon. It is lighter in color, thinner and more expensive, and can be found in stick form in Hispanic grocery or specialty shops. Grind it in a *molcajete* or spice grinder. Cassia bark has a stronger flavor than Mexican cinnamon, but makes an acceptable substitute. Do not use ground cinnamon as a substitute where cinnamon sticks are called for.

Mexican oregano is actually wild marjoram (*Lippia graveolens*), distinctly different from European or Greek oregano (*Origanum vulgare*). It can be used fresh or dry.

Nopales are spineless cactus leaves from the genus *Opuntia*. They are chopped or cut into strips and used fresh in salads or cooked as a vegetable. They have a slightly tart green bean flavor.

Pepitas are dried and roasted squash or pumpkin seeds; they are salted and eaten as a snack or used in chile sauces.

Pickled jalapeños chiles are milder in flavor than the fresh variety and are typically offered as a condiment in New Mexican cuisine. They can be found whole, sliced and chopped in cans and bottles in most well-stocked supermarkets. Refrigerate pickled jalapeños after opening.

Piloncillo is unrefined sugar that is sold in cone shapes. It has a slight flavor of molasses and is primarily used in baking.

Pimientos (the Spanish word for peppers) are heart-shaped sweet red peppers, similar to the bell pepper but more aromatic. They are most widely used as a stuffing for green olives, and they add color and flavor to soups, salads and vegetable side dishes. Pimientos are available jarred in most supermarkets.

Piñon nuts, or pine nuts, are small elongated ivory-colored seeds collected from pine cones of the stone pine trees. When raw, the seeds have a soft texture and a sweet, buttery flavor. They are often lightly toasted to bring out the flavor and to add a crunchy texture. Piñon nuts are harvested by hand and are therefore quite expensive. They can be found in most well-stocked supermarkets.

Pomegranate molasses, also known as pomegranate concentrate, is a thick reddish brown syrup made from the reduced juice of fresh pomegranates. A staple in the Middle Eastern, prepared pomegranate molasses is available in Middle Eastern food stores. You can also make you own with the following recipe:

3 cups (750 ml) pomegranate juice
$1/2$ cup (100 g) sugar
$1/2$ cup (125 ml) freshly squeezed lemon juice

Combine all the ingredients in a saucepan and heat over medium heat, stirring until the sugar is dissolved. Reduce the heat and simmer the syrup until it reduces to 1 cup (125 ml), about 45 minutes. Cool and store the syrup in the refrigerator.

Prickly pear cactus juice is made from the spiny red fruits of the prickly pear cactus, the same cactus from which nopales are harvested. Prickly pear jellies and syrup are made from this bountiful plant as well as a vitamin rich juice that makes a wonderful addition to sauces, drinks and desserts. Bottled prickly pear cactus juice can be found in Hispanic grocery stores and specialty shops.

Quelites, also called lamb's-quarters, are wild edible greens used in a variety of recipes. They are most commonly sautéed with garlic and chilies and served with beans, or sautéed with onions and garlic and then folded into a soft tortilla to make a quelites taco. Quelites can be hard to find, but fresh spinach, chard or kale can be substituted.

Quinoa, the seed of the Goosefoot plant, is used as a grain in New Mexican cooking. Reverend for its nutritionl value, quinoa's delicate, crunchy texture and nutty flavor make it a perfect filling for chiles and a versatile side dish. Quinoa can be found at health food stores and well-stocked supermarkets.

Saffron is the world's most expensive spice. The dried strands should be allowed to infuse in warm milk before being added to rice and dessert dishes. Store saffron in the freezer as it loses its fragrance quickly, and never buy powdered saffron if you want the true aroma of this spice.

Scallions, also known as spring onions, are actually the immature stalks of onions. They have long green leaves and a small white bulb. Both parts are edible. When cooked or raw, they have a pleasant mild flavor. Use as a substitute for **Mexican bulb onions**.

Tequila is a colorless or pale Mexican liquor that is made by fermenting and distilling the sap of the agave plant. It is used in many cocktails, the best known being the margarita. As with other hard alcohols, there are many different ages, styles and mixes of tequila. The drink recipes included in this book recommend specific tequilas, but you can experiment with different ones to create your own signature margarita.

Tomatillos are a small, green relative of the tomato and are sometimes called *tomate verde*. They are tart and have a light brown outer covering, or husk, that must be removed before using. They should be firm; never use soft tomatillos.

Tortillas are round, flat, unleavened bread made from corn or wheat flour and lard, and cooked on a griddle. While corn tortillas are fried crisp for nachos, tacos, tostadas and enchiladas, flour tortillas are often wrapped around fillings to make burritos and are served alongside fajitas, soups and stews. Both varieties are available readymade at supermarkets. They come in various sizes and may contain flavors like spinach or red pepper.

Zucchini (courgettes) are at their best in spring. Look for firm-fleshed zucchini that have not been punctured. Female zucchini are sometimes sold with their yellow flowers still attached. These are completely edible and make a lovely garnish.

Authentic Santa Fe Recipes

Sauces and Salsas

Roasted Corn and Black Bean Salsa

Serve this colorful dish chilled as a salsa or warmed as a side dish or vegetable.

2 ears fresh corn, or $1/2$ cup (100 g) canned or frozen whole-kernel corn, defrosted
1 medium-sized tomato, chopped
1 small red onion, chopped
$1/2$ cup (40 g) cooked black beans, rinsed
4 tablespoons chopped green or red bell pepper (capsicum)
2 jalapeño chiles, deseeded and diced
1 clove garlic, minced
1 teaspoon oregano, preferably Mexican
$1/4$ teaspoon cumin seeds
3 tablespoons olive oil
2 tablespoons freshly squeezed lime juice
Salt to taste

1 If using fresh corn, cut the kernels off the cobs. Roast them over high heat in a dry, heavy skillet for a couple of minutes, or until the kernels are slightly browned, stirring constantly. Remove from the heat.
2 Combine the corn, tomato, onion, black beans, pepper, jalapeños chiles, garlic, oregano and cumin, and gently mix. Whisk the oil and lime juice together, pour over the salsa and gently toss. Allow the salsa to sit for an hour to blend the flavors before serving.

Makes $2^1/2$ to 3 cups
Preparation time: 30 mins + 1 hour to develop flavor

Green Tomatillo Sauce
Salsa Verde

Tomatillos, Mexican husk-tomatoes or *tomates verdes*, aren't tomatoes and don't even taste like them. They have a tangy, citrus-like taste that can be very tart. This sauce can be used with and on other foods, or it can be served as a salsa with chips.

1 lb (500 g) tomatillos, husks removed, chopped, or 1 can (11 oz/300 g) tomatillos, drained
$1/2$ cup (75 g) diced white onion
2 cloves garlic, minced
2 or 3 serrano chiles (seeds included), minced
4 tablespoons chopped cilantro (coriander leaves)
Sugar and salt to taste

1 Combine the tomatillos, onion, garlic and chiles in a pan. Simmer over low heat for a couple of minutes, until the tomatillos are soft but still colorful. Add sugar and salt to taste.
2 For a chunky sauce, stir in the cilantro and serve. Otherwise, put the sauce in a blender or food processor and purée until smooth. Add the cilantro and serve.

Notes: If serving the sauce as a fresh salsa, combine all the ingredients in a bowl. Add sugar and salt to taste. Allow the salsa to sit for an hour before serving to blend the flavors.

Makes 2 to $2^1/2$ cups (500 to 750 ml)
Preparation time: 15 mins
Cooking time: 5 mins

Chile Piquín Salsa

This salsa is served either smooth or with texture. It's best made with fully ripe tomatoes, but canned tomatoes may be substituted. In fact, the flavor is better with canned tomatoes than with unripe ones.

2 tablespoons crushed piquín chile, seeds included
1 cup (250 ml) hot water
6 plum tomatoes, chopped, or 1 can (1 lb/500 g) diced tomatoes
1 can (250 ml) tomato sauce
1 small onion, chopped
1 tablespoon red wine vinegar
1 teaspoon garlic powder
2 teaspoons sugar
Pinch of ground cumin
Pinch of oregano, preferably Mexican
Salt to taste

1 In a mixing bowl, cover the chile with the hot water and steep for several minutes.
2 In a saucepan over medium heat, combine the remaining ingredients, the chile and the water in which the chile soaked and simmer for five minutes. If the salsa is too thick, thin it with water or broth to the desired consistency. Add salt to taste. Allow the salsa to sit at room temperature for an hour to blend the flavors.

Makes 2 cups
Preparation time: 20 mins + 1 hour to develop flavor
Cooking time: 5 mins

Chile Colorado

The chiles that are traditionally used for this sauce are the ones on ristras (strings of chiles). Stringing chiles is not just for decoration; it is a method of drying and preserving the chile crop for use throughout the year. Use this sauce in a number of dishes, as a topping for enchiladas and tacos, as a basis for stew—anything that calls for a red sauce.

10 to 12 dried New Mexican red
  chiles
1 medium-sized onion, chopped
2 cloves garlic, chopped
2 tablespoons oil
2 cups (500 ml) water or broth
1 teaspoon oregano, preferably
  Mexican
Pinch of ground cumin
Salt to taste

1 Arrange the chile pods on a baking pan and place them in a 250°F (120°C, gas mark $1/2$) oven for 10 to 15 minutes, or until the chiles become very aromatic—do not let them burn.
2 Remove the stems and seeds and crumble the pods into a saucepan. Cover the chiles with very hot water and allow them to steep for 15 to 20 minutes to soften. Drain them and remove from the pan.
3 Sauté the onion and garlic in the oil until soft. Add the chiles and water or broth and simmer for 10 minutes. Remove from the heat.
4 Place all the ingredients in a blender or food processor and purée them until smooth. Strain the mixture for a smoother sauce. If the sauce is too thin, place it back on the stove and simmer until it is reduced to the desired consistency, or if too thick, add more water or broth. Adjust the seasonings and serve.

Makes $2^1/2$ to 3 cups (625 to 750 ml)
Preparation time: 30 mins
Cooking time: 30 mins

Chipotle Sauce

Chipotles, smoked dried jalapeños, originated in the ancient civilization of Teotihuacán, near Mexico City, centuries before the Aztecs. The distinctive smoky and slightly sweet taste of these chiles adds layers of flavor to any sauce or dish. A word of caution: These chiles are hot and strong flavored; adding too many can overpower and overheat a dish, so start with a few and then add more until you reach the desired level of spiciness.

4 dried chipotle chiles
2 dried New Mexican red chiles
1 small onion, chopped
1 tablespoon oil
4 medium-sized tomatoes, peeled
  and chopped, or 1 can (1lb/500 g)
  diced tomatoes
1 cup (250 ml) beef broth
3 tablespoons cider vinegar
1 tablespoon brown sugar
$1/2$ teaspoon salt
$1/4$ teaspoon ground white pepper
$1/4$ teaspoon ground cumin

1 Place the chiles in a large bowl and cover them with hot water. Steep until they're soft, 15 to 20 minutes. Drain the chiles and discard the water. Remove the stems and chop the chiles.
2 In a saucepan, sauté the onion in the oil until it's soft but not brown. Add the chiles and the remaining ingredients and simmer for 15 to 20 minutes to thicken. Remove from the heat.
3 Purée all the ingredients in a blender or food processor until smooth (don't strain).

Makes 3 cups (750 ml)
Preparation time: 15 mins
Cooking time: 25 mins

Green Chile Sauce

This is another classic sauce that is basic to the cuisine of Santa Fe. It is lightly flavored, with a pungency that ranges from medium to mild depending on the heat of the chiles. Adding finely diced pork or beef, omitting the tomatoes, and thickening with a roux of flour and oil are all popular variations.

2 tablespoons oil
1 small onion, chopped
1 clove garlic, minced
8 to 10 New Mexican green chiles,
  roasted, peeled and chopped
1 small tomato, peeled and chopped
3 cups (750 ml) chicken or vegetable
  broth
$1/4$ teaspoon ground cumin
2 tablespoons cornstarch mixed with
  3 tablespoons water

1 In a saucepan over medium heat, sauté the onion and garlic in the oil until soft. Add the chiles, tomato, 2 cups (500 ml) of the broth and cumin. Bring the sauce to a boil, reduce the heat, and simmer for 10 minutes.
2 Stir in the cornstarch mixture and continue to simmer for an additional 5 to 10 minutes to thicken. Add more broth to thin the mixture if the sauce becomes too thick. Adjust the seasonings and serve.

Makes 2 to $2^1/2$ cups (500 to 625 ml)
Preparation time: 30 mins
Cooking time: 30 mins

New Mexican Green Chile Salsa

This salsa is best made with fresh New Mexican chiles.

4 to 5 New Mexican green chiles, roasted, peeled and chopped
2 jalapeño chiles, diced
1 medium-sized red onion, diced
3 cloves garlic, minced
2 tablespoons chopped cilantro (coriander leaves)
1 teaspoon minced fresh oregano
1 can (1 lb/500 g) diced tomatoes, drained
Salt to taste

Combine all the ingredients in a bowl and allow to sit for an hour at room temperature before serving.

Makes 2 to 2$^1/_2$ cups
Preparation time: 15 mins + 1 hour to develop flavor

Other Basics

Taco or Tostada Shells

Oil, for frying
12 corn tortillas

1 To prepare taco shells, fill a heavy skillet with the oil to a depth of 1 in (2$^1/_2$ cm) and heat until hot. Test by dipping a tiny piece of tortilla in the oil: if small bubbles rise, the oil is ready.
2 Using a pair of tongs, dip the tortilla into the oil for 5 to 10 seconds. Fold the tortilla in half and hold it open while it cooks, to shape one side. When the tortilla is crisp, after about 20 seconds, turn it over and cook the other side. Be sure to hold the taco open so there will be room for the filling. Remove and drain on paper towels.
3 To make tostada shells, follow the same procedure, but make a small slit in the center of the tortilla and don't fold it.

Makes 12   Preparation time: 5 mins
Cooking time: 15 mins

Pickled Red Onions   Sante Fe School of Cooking

This recipe requires advance preparation.

2 cups (500 ml) red wine vinegar
1 can (6 oz/185 ml) frozen orange juice concentrate, thawed
$^3/_4$ cup (150 g) sugar
1 tablespoon dried oregano, preferably Mexican
4 bay leaves, broken in half
Salt to taste
1$^1/_4$ lbs (625 g) medium-sized red onions (about 6), cut into slivers

1 Combine all the ingredients, except the onions, in a large nonreactive bowl and stir until the sugar has dissolved.
2 Add the onions and combine them well. Cover the bowl and let the mixture stand at room temperature, stirring occasionally, for 12 to 24 hours. Stir the mixture once again, cover the bowl, and refrigerate.

Makes 4 cups   Preparation time: 15 mins

Saffron Rice

1 teaspoon saffron threads
2 cups (400 g) uncooked white rice
$^1/_4$ cup (60 ml) olive oil
$^1/_2$ white onion, minced
2 teaspoons minced garlic
1$^1/_2$ teaspoons kosher salt
$^1/_2$ teaspoon ground white pepper

1 Toast the saffron in a small, dry sauté pan over medium heat, shaking the pan continuously to prevent burning. Toast for 2 minutes, or until fragrant. Remove the saffron from the heat and reserve it.
2 Wash the rice in a couple of changes of water until the water runs clear, then drain. Set aside.
3 In a large saucepan over medium heat, combine the oil, onion, garlic, salt and pepper. Stir for 1 to 2 minutes and add the washed rice. Stir constantly until the oil is absorbed and the rice begins to smell nutty, about 2 minutes. Add 3 cups (750 ml) of water to the rice, stir in the saffron, and bring to a boil over medium-high heat. Reduce the heat to low, cover the saucepan, and simmer until all the water is absorbed, 20 to 30 minutes.

Serves 8 to 10   Preparation time: 10 mins   Cooking time: 35 mins

Corn Chips with Melted Cheese, Chiles and Pinto Beans   Nachos

There are numerous variations of these popular appetizers. Nachos is another one of those dishes that you can vary to suit your tastes. Change the type of beans or cheese, add chorizo, change the chile, or even substitute crabmeat. There are no rules.

5 oz (150 g) tortilla chips, yellow, red, blue or a combination of all three
$^1/_2$ cup (40 g) cooked pinto beans, drained
4 tablespoons sliced pickled jalapeño chiles, drained
2 to 3 tablespoons sliced black olives
2 cups (250 g) grated Cheddar cheese
Chopped fresh cilantro (coriander leaves), to garnish
Sour cream (optional), to serve

Guacamole
3 very ripe avocados, preferably Haas
1 small tomato, finely diced
4 tablespoons minced white onion
2 serrano chiles, minced
1 clove garlic, minced
2 teaspoons freshly squeezed lime or lemon juice
Salt to taste

1 Prepare the Guacamole by cubing the avocados and placing them in a large bowl. Crush the avocado cubes with a fork or a masher until they're almost smooth but still retain a little texture. Mix in the remaining ingredients. Allow the Guacamole to sit for an hour to blend the flavors before serving. This makes about $1^1/_2$ cups of Guacamole salsa.
2 Preheat the oven to 400°F (200°C, gas mark 6). Arrange the tortillas on a pan or ovenproof plate. Sprinkle the beans, chiles, olives and cheese over the chips and bake in the oven or under the broiler until the cheese melts, 3 to 5 minutes. Remove from the oven, garnish with the cilantro and top with Guacamole and sour cream if desired. Serve immediately with additional sauces on the side.

Notes: To prevent the Guacamole from turning black, squeeze a little lemon juice on the top. Cover with plastic wrap pressed into the surface so there are no air pockets. Another way is to put the avocado pit in the Guacamole before covering it. Although there is some contention about whether this works, I always do it. To prepare the nachos in a microwave oven, use a microwavable plate and microwave on high for 3 to 4 minutes. To make homemade chips, cut corn tortillas into wedges and fry them in 400°F (200°C) oil until crisp. Remove them from the oil and drain on paper towels.

Serves 4 to 6   Preparation time: 30 mins + 1 hour to develop flavor
Cooking time: 5 mins

Goat Cheese and Roast Pepper Quesadillas   Santa Fe School of Cooking

Quesadillas are stuffed flour tortilla turnovers that can be toasted, fried, or baked—a type of Southwestern or Mexican sandwich. These appetizers or snacks can be filled with just about any mixture, but cheese is the most common filling. In this recipe, the quesadillas are open rather than folded.

8 flour tortillas (each 8 in/20 cm)
2 cups (250 g) grated Monterey Jack cheese
1 cup (200 g) crumbled goat cheese
3 tablespoons olive oil
1 medium-sized onion, thinly sliced
2 cloves garlic, thinly sliced
1 red bell pepper (capsicum), roasted and cut into thin strips
1 yellow bell pepper (capsicum), roasted and cut into thin strips
1 or 2 New Mexican green chiles, roasted, peeled, deseeded and cut into thin strips
Salt to taste
Freshly ground black pepper to taste
Fresh basil or oregano (optional)

1 Preheat the oven to 350°F (180°C, gas mark 4). Place the tortillas on a flat surface and sprinkle each one with 4 tablespoons of Jack cheese. Sprinkle 1 tablespoon of goat cheese over the Jack cheese.
2 Heat the oil in a large skillet over medium-high heat. Add the onion and sauté until it is translucent. Add the garlic and continue to cook until the garlic is just golden. Add the red and yellow pepper strips, and the chile strips, combining them thoroughly. Season with the salt and pepper to taste.
3 Divide the sautéed ingredients among the tortillas and top with additional goat cheese.
4 Bake the quesadillas in the oven for 10 to 12 minutes, or until the cheese melts. Remove them from the oven and cut each quesadilla into 4 pieces and serve warm.

Serves 4 to 6   Preparation time: 20 mins   Cooking time: 30 mins

Lobster Ceviche with Plantain Chips   Mark Kiffin, Coyote Cafe

This version of ceviche uses lobster meat instead of the traditional scallops, shrimp, and squids. It is important to use the freshest seafood to make a quality ceviche.

2 lobsters, cooked and shelled (1$^1/_2$ lbs/750 g each)
1 medium-sized tomato, diced
1 medium-sized red onion, diced
1 cucumber, peeled, deseeded and diced
Freshly squeezed juice of 2 limes
1 teaspoon habanero sauce
$^1/_2$ teaspoon salt
1 teaspoon olive oil
2 avocados, diced
Fresh cilantro (coriander leaves) sprigs, to garnish

Plantain Chips
Oil, for frying
2 green plantains, thinly sliced lengthwise
Salt to taste
Freshly squeezed juice of 1 lime

1 Slice the lobster meat, toss with the tomato, onion, cucumber, lime juice, habanero sauce, salt and olive oil. Chill in the refrigerator for half an hour to 1 hour.
2 To make the Plantain Chips, heat the oil to 300°F (150°C). Fry the plantains until they're crisp but not dark. Remove from the oil, drain and season them with the salt and lime juice while they're still warm.
3 To assemble, toss the lobster mixture with the diced avocado or layer them in a tall sundae glass. Garnish with cilantro sprigs and Plantain Chips and serve.

Serves 6   Preparation time: 30 mins + 1 hour to chill   Cooking time: 10 mins

Spicy Sautéed Shrimp   Gambas Al Ajillo

Tapas, or hors d'oeuvres, are the "little bites" or small portions of dishes that are served with cocktails in the bars and taverns of Spain. Tapas can be eaten as an appetizer, or an assortment can be eaten as a meal.

1/4 cup (60 ml) olive oil
4 whole garlic cloves plus 1 tablespoon minced garlic
14 oz (400 g) fresh medium-sized
   shrimp, peeled and deveined
2 tablespoons freshly squeezed lime
   juice
2 tablespoons butter
1/2 teaspoon ground paprika
Pinch of crushed piquín chile
1/3 cup (90 ml) lamb or beef stock,
   lightly seasoned with a pinch of
   ground cloves, cinnamon and dried
   thyme
2 tablespoons dry Madeira or port
   wine
Salt to taste
Freshly ground black pepper to taste
2 tablespoons coarsely chopped
   fresh Italian parsley

1 In a large sauté pan or a heavy-bottomed pan, heat the olive oil with the whole garlic cloves over the highest heat until smoking. Add the shrimp and quickly turn them over and cook for a few seconds to seal in the flavor. Remove the pan from the heat.
2 Pour out all of the oil and discard the garlic. Return the shrimp to the pan over medium-high heat. Pour the lime juice over the shrimp and add the butter, minced garlic, paprika, piquín, lamb or beef stock, and Madeira. Simmer until the shrimp turn pink, a couple of minutes. Season with the salt and pepper.
3 Toss the dish with the parsley and serve immediately.

Note: If you substitute port wine for Madeira, the sauce will be as rich and the dish tastes just as good.

Serves 4   Preparation time: 20 mins   Cooking time: 5 mins

Ceviche

In ceviche, raw fish is "cooked" without heat, through a chemical reaction with an acid, such as lime juice. The flavors in this dish cleanse the palate.

1 lb (500 g) shucked bay scallops
8 oz (250 g) fresh shrimp, peeled
   and deveined
8 oz (250 g) fresh small squids, ten-
   tacles separated, body cut into rings
2 scallions (spring onions), thinly
   sliced to yield about 1 cup
1 bunch fresh cilantro (coriander
   leaves), finely chopped to yield
   about 1/2 cup
1 large jalapeño chile, chopped
2 1/2 cups (625 ml) freshly squeezed
   lime juice

Place all the ingredients except the lime juice in a non-reactive bowl. Pour the juice over the mixture to cover. Marinate in the refrigerator for 2 hours. Serve the ceviche chilled.

Serves 6 to 8   Preparation time: 30 mins + 2 hours to marinate

Clockwise from top: Moroccan Eggplant with Cilantro Pesto (page 38), Sautéed Wild Mushrooms with Spaghetti Squash (page 38), Spanish Tortilla (page 39), Ceviche and Spicy Sautéed Shrimp.

Sautéed Wild Mushrooms with Spaghetti Squash

1 spaghetti squash (about 2 lbs/1 kg)
3 tablespoons unsalted butter
1 tablespoon olive oil
1 slice uncooked bacon, diced
8 oz (250 g) sliced wild mushrooms,
   such as oyster or portobello
1 scallion (spring onion), sliced
2 tablespoons medium-sweet sherry
4 tablespoons lamb or beef stock
Salt to taste
Freshly ground black pepper to taste
Chopped fresh Italian parsley,
   to garnish

Serves 6 to 8
Preparation time: 15 mins
Cooking time: 40 mins

1 Preheat the oven to 450°F (230°C, gas mark 8). Cut the squash in half lengthwise, scoop out the seeds, and rub the butter over the squash. Place on a baking pan lined with aluminum foil. Bake for 30 to 40 minutes, or until the squash is tender.
2 In a sauté pan over medium-low heat, add the oil and bacon and cook until all the fat has been rendered from the bacon. Add the mushrooms and scallion and toss until coated. Sauté until the scallion is tender and slightly browned, 3 to 5 minutes. Raise the heat and add the sherry. Reduce the heat, stir in the lamb or beef stock, and heat through a couple of minutes. Season to taste with salt and pepper.
3 To serve, pull the long strands out of the squash with a fork and place them on a serving plate. Spoon the mushroom mixture over the squash, garnish with the parsley, and serve at once.

Moroccan Eggplant with Cilantro Pesto

1 large or 2 small eggplants
   (aubergines)
1/2 teaspoon oil
1 red bell (capsicum) or pimiento
   pepper, roasted, peeled and thinly
   sliced
2 teaspoons coarsely chopped Italian
   parsley
4 to 6 tablespoons olive oil
Black olives, to serve

Cilantro Pesto
1 large bunch (2 cups/150 g) fresh
   cilantro (coriander leaves), stems
   removed
1/4 cup (60 ml) freshly squeezed
   lemon juice
1/2 cup (125 ml) olive oil
1/2 teaspoon ground cumin
Salt to taste

Serves 6
Preparation time: 15 mins
Cooking time: 45 mins

1 Preheat oven to 375°F (190°C, gas mark 5). Pierce the eggplants with a fork and coat with the oil. Place on a baking pan and bake for 25 minutes. Turn over and continue to cook for an additional 20 minutes, or until it is only slightly firm. Remove from the oven and allow to cool to room temperature.
2 To make the Cilantro Pesto, thoroughly clean the cilantro and chop it in a food processor. While it's processing, gradually add the remaining ingredients until the mixture is a deep green, aromatic purée.
3 When the eggplants have cooled enough to handle, remove the skin and try to remove most of the seeds with a fork, but don't sacrifice good eggplant meat to be seed-free. Coarsely chop the eggplants into bite-sized chunks and place them neatly in a shallow earthenware or glass pan for serving.
4 Garnish with roasted red pepper, sprinkle on the parsley, and coat lightly with the olive oil. Serve accompanied with individual bowls of Cilantro Pesto and black olives.

Spanish Tortilla   Tortilla Española

A traditional tapa, this Spanish omelet is made with potatoes and eggs and is served, at room temperature, with Romesco Sauce.

3 lbs (1¹/₂ kg) potatoes (approximately 10 medium-sized potatoes), peeled and sliced into ¹/₈-in (¹/₃-cm) thick slices
¹/₃ cup (90 ml) olive oil
1 medium-sized onion, thinly sliced
6 eggs, beaten
¹/₄ teaspoon salt

Romesco Sauce
³/₄ cup (100 g) toasted almonds
10 cloves garlic
¹/₂ cup (125 ml) olive oil
¹/₄ cup (60 ml) red wine vinegar
2 to 3 dried piquín chiles
2 red bell peppers (capsicum), roasted, peeled and deseeded
Salt to taste

1 Preheat the oven to 350°F (180°C, gas mark 4). In a small roasting pan, toss the potatoes with the oil, cover, and bake for 20 minutes. Uncover the pan and spread the onion slices evenly over the potatoes. Cover and bake for an additional 10 minutes, or until the potatoes are just done. Remove the pan and pour off the oil, reserving it. Cool the potatoes to room temperature.
2 To prepare the Romesco Sauce, purée the almonds, garlic, oil, vinegar and chiles in a blender or food processor until smooth. Add the peppers, replace the top, and pulse until the sauce is just a bit chunky. Salt to taste.
3 Season the eggs with the salt. Gently fold the potato-and-onion mixture into the eggs and mix carefully.
4 Heat a nonstick sauté pan over high heat with a few tablespoons of the reserved oil. When it's hot, carefully add the egg mixture. Allow the eggs to set on a high heat for a minute while gently shaking the pan so they don't stick. Reduce the heat to the lowest temperature and cook for 15 to 20 minutes, or until the mixture is firm. Remove from the heat.
5 Place a plate on top (upside down as you look at it) of the sauté pan and flip the tortilla onto the plate. (Do this over your sink.) Reheat the skillet over high heat and carefully slide the tortilla back into the pan. Reduce the heat to low and cook the other side until it's done, about 8 minutes. When the tortilla feels firm to the touch, it's done.
6 Cool the tortilla to room temperature and slice it into wedges. When you are ready to serve the tortilla, spoon some of the Romesco Sauce onto a plate and place a wedge on top.

Serves 6   Preparation time: 30 mins   Cooking time: 45 mins

Grilled Swordfish Tacos   Mark Kiffin, Coyote Cafe

These tacos are served with an unusual salsa. Huitlacoche is available frozen or in cans; either may be used in this recipe. Large scallions can be substituted for the Mexican bulb onions.

Corn and Huitlacoche Salsa
1 tablespoon peanut oil
$^1/_2$ cup (75 g) minced white onion
4 serrano chiles, roasted, peeled and chopped, seeds included
4 cloves garlic, roasted and mashed
2 cups (300 g) huitlacoche
5 plum tomatoes, diced
1 teaspoon minced fresh epazote
12 cilantro (coriander) leaves
$^1/_2$ teaspoon salt
1 ear fresh corn, kernels cut off the cob
1 teaspoon *chipotles en adobo sauce*
3 lbs (1$^1/_2$ kg) swordfish, sliced into 3 large pieces
1 lb (500 g) Mexican bulb onions
18 white corn tortillas (each 6 in/15 cm)
Sprigs of cilantro (coriander leaves), to garnish
2 limes, sliced, to serve

Cracked Coriander and Black Pepper Rub
4 tablespoons coriander seeds
2 tablespoons dried oregano
1 tablespoon black peppercorns
$^1/_2$ teaspoon sugar
$^1/_4$ teaspoon salt

1 Prepare the Corn and Huitlacoche Salsa by heating the oil in a sauté pan. Add the onion, serrano chiles and garlic, and cook for 2 minutes to soften. Add the huitlacoche, tomatoes, epazote, cilantro and salt, and continue cooking for 15 minutes.
2 Soften the corn by placing it in a separate pan, adding 2 tablespoons of water, and cooking until the water has evaporated. Stir in the *chipotles en adobo,* and then add the corn mixture to the huitlacoche mixture. Adjust the seasonings to taste.
3 Prepare the Cracked Coriander and Black Pepper Rub by placing all the ingredients in a dry skillet and toasting them over medium heat for 2 minutes, or until fragrant. Transfer the mixture to a spice grinder and grind until smooth.
4 Heat a grill. Rub the swordfish slices with the Cracked Coriander and Black Pepper Rub and grill the fish along with the bulb onions to desired doneness, about 8 minutes.
5 Soften the tortillas by dipping them in warm water and placing them on the grill or a hot pan. They will steam and soften.
6 To serve, slice the grilled swordfish into 18 to 24 pieces, allowing 3 to 4 pieces for each taco. Slice the grilled onions and place them in the tacos along with the fish. Stack three tacos on a plate and garnish with cilantro sprigs and lime. Place the Corn and Huitlacoche Salsa on top or around the tacos and serve at once.

Serves 6   Preparation time: 45 mins   Cooking time: 35 mins

Catalan Pancakes with Lobster and Crab
Maurice Zeck, La Fonda

A Santa Fe version of pancakes from the Spanish region of Catalonia.

5 oz (150 g) fresh small shrimp, peeled and deveined
5 oz (150 g) lobster meat
5 oz (150 g) Dungeness crabmeat
1 tablespoon chopped shallots
$^1/_2$ cup (125 ml) white wine

Roasted Red Pepper Sauce
2 teaspoons clarified butter
1 tablespoon chopped shallots
1 large (8 oz/250 g) red bell peppers (capsicum), roasted, peeled, and puréed
$^1/_4$ cup (60 ml) broth reserved from the seafood
2 tablespoons cornstarch mixed with 3 tablespoons water
Salt and ground white pepper to taste

Pancakes
2 eggs
$^1/_2$ cup (75 g) flour
$^1/_4$ cup (60 ml) milk
$^1/_2$ teaspoon salt
$^1/_4$ teaspoon ground white pepper
4 tablespoons finely diced red bell pepper (capsicum)
5 tablespoons chopped fresh cilantro (coriander leaves)
2 scallions (spring onions), sliced

1 Combine the seafood, shallots and wine in a sauté pan. Cover the pan and place over low heat until the seafood has released its juices and the shallots are soft but not browned. Strain off the broth and reserve it.
2 To make the Roasted Red Pepper Sauce, heat the butter in a saucepan, add the shallots, and sauté until they are soft but not browned, 3 to 5 minutes. Add the bell pepper purée and broth and bring to a boil. Reduce the heat and simmer for 5 minutes. Slowly stir in just enough of the cornstarch mixture to thicken the sauce. Add salt and pepper to taste.
3 To make the Pancakes, mix the eggs, flour, remaining seafood broth, milk, salt and pepper to a batter in a large bowl. Stir in the red pepper, 3 tablespoons of the cilantro, the scallions and seafood.
4 Heat a lightly oiled griddle until hot. Form silver-dollar-sized pancakes and bake them on the griddle until they're cooked through, 3 to 4 minutes for each side, turning them only once.
5 To serve, arrange 3 pancakes on a plate and top with the Roasted Red Pepper Sauce. Garnish the pancakes with the remaining cilantro and serve at once.

Note: To clarify butter, heat it in a saucepan or in a microwave oven, to separate the oil from the solids, and refrigerate. When it solidifies, discard the bottom sediment.

Serves 4 to 6   Preparation time: 45 mins   Cooking time: 1 hour

Blue Crab Cakes   Paul Hunsicker, Paul's Restaurant of Santa Fe

At Paul's, they serve these crab cakes with a delicious Tomato-orange Chipotle Sauce.

2 cups (250 g) cooked crabmeat,
  either fresh or canned, picked over
  for bits of shell
3 eggs, beaten
1 cup (30 g) chopped fresh parsley
$^1/_2$ cup (125 ml) Dijon mustard
2 cups (120 g) breadcrumbs
$^1/_4$ cup (60 ml) olive oil

Tomato-orange Chipotle Sauce
2 cups (450 g) chopped tomatoes
3 oranges, peeled, sectioned with
  membranes removed, finely chopped
1 red onion, finely chopped
4 tablespoons finely chopped fresh
  cilantro (coriander leaves)
3 chipotles en adobo, finely chopped
1 cup (250 ml) white wine
2 tablespoons butter
Salt and pepper to taste
Red, yellow, and green bell pepper
  (capsicum) slices, to garnish

1 In a large mixing bowl, combine the crabmeat, eggs, parsley, mustard and bread crumbs. Mix well and let stand a few minutes to blend the flavors.
2 Form the crab mixture into 2-oz (60-g) cakes. Heat the oil in a sauté pan over medium-high heat until very hot. Add the cakes, a few at a time, and pan-fry them until they are well browned on both sides, turning only once. Remove from the oil and drain them on paper towels.
3 To make the Tomato-orange Chipotle Sauce, combine the tomatoes, oranges, onion, cilantro, chipotles en adobo and wine in the pan in which the cakes were cooked. Bring the mixture to a boil, add the butter, and season with the salt and pepper.
4 Arrange a couple of crab cakes on a plate, spread the sauce on top, garnish with bell pepper slices, and serve immediately.

Serves 4   Preparation time: 30 mins   Cooking time: 30 mins

Garlic Soup

With its roots in both Spain and Mexico, this version of a classic soup uses bread as a thickener. The garlic should be cooked very slowly so that it is soft and "creamy," not browned. The amount of garlic may be adjusted to suit your tastes.

$^1/_4$ cup (60 ml) olive oil
9 cloves garlic, thinly sliced
2 slices French bread, crusts removed, cubed
4 cups (1 liter) chicken broth
1 sprig fresh epazote
Salt and freshly ground black pepper to taste
4 eggs, beaten
Chopped cilantro (coriander leaves) or parsley, to garnish
Lime wedges, to serve

1 Heat a heavy skillet over medium-low heat, add the oil and garlic, and sauté gently until the garlic is golden, about 5 minutes. Remove the garlic from the oil and reserve it. Return the pan to the heat and sauté the bread until golden.
2 Place the garlic and bread in a saucepan over medium heat. Add the broth and epazote, cover, and simmer until the bread breaks down and mixes with the broth, 10 to 15 minutes. Season to taste with the salt and pepper. Raise the heat and stir in the eggs until they are cooked.
3 Garnish the soup with cilantro and serve it immediately with lime wedges on the side.

Serves 4   Preparation time: 15 mins   Cooking time: 25 mins

Black Bean Soup   Rosalea Murphy, The Pink Adobe Restaurant

Turtle beans, or black beans, are native to South America. Their slightly mushroom-like flavor enhances dishes throughout South and Central America, the Caribbean and New Mexico. If you don't have time to soak the beans overnight, substituting canned beans also works well.

1 cup (200 g) dried black beans, soaked overnight
$1/2$ green bell pepper (capsicum), or 4 to 5 fresh New Mexican green chiles, roasted, peeled and chopped to yield about $1/2$ cup
2 tablespoons olive oil
$11/2$ large onions, chopped
2 cloves garlic, minced
12 oz (350 g) ham hock
4 cups (1 liter) beef broth
$11/2$ teaspoons ground cumin
$11/2$ teaspoons dried oregano
$1/4$ teaspoon dried thyme
$1/2$ bay leaf
4 tablespoons chopped pickled jalapeño chiles
1 tablespoon dry sherry
Salt and freshly ground black pepper to taste

Garnishes
Diced tomato
Sliced scallions (spring onions)
Sliced hard-boiled eggs
Sour cream

1 Wash the beans and place them in a stockpot along with the bell pepper or green chiles. Add enough water to cover the ingredients, and soak them overnight, then drain.

2 Heat the oil in a heavy skillet, add the onion and garlic, and sauté for 3 minutes over medium heat.

3 Combine the onion mixture, bean mixture and ham hock in a large stockpot and cover them with the broth. Raise the heat to just below boiling, then reduce the heat and simmer for 1 hour. Add the herbs, jalapeños and sherry, and season with the salt and pepper. Continue to cook for an additional $11/2$ hours, or until the beans are done. To thicken the soup, remove about $1/2$ cup (50 g) beans from the pot, mash them, and return them to the pot. Stir well and adjust the seasonings to taste.

4 To serve, ladle the soup into individual bowls. Garnish with the tomato, scallions, eggs, and sour cream, and serve immediately.

Serves 4 to 5   Preparation time: 30 mins + overnight soaking
Cooking time: 2 hours 30 mins

Mexican Corn Chowder   Rosalea Murphy, The Pink Adobe Restaurant

4 oz (125 g) butter (1 stick)
$1/2$ cup (50 g) sliced mushrooms
1 green bell pepper (capsicum), diced
1 large onion, diced
1 jalapeño chile, diced
1 teaspoon cumin seed
$3/4$ cup (90 g) flour
1 teaspoon ground paprika
1 teaspoon ground red pepper
4 cups (1 liter) chicken broth
2 cups (500 ml) half-and-half (pouring cream)
$1/2$ cup (60 g) grated Cheddar cheese
1 can (17 oz/550 g) whole-kernel corn
1 tablespoon chopped fresh parsley
1 tablespoon diced pimiento
Salt to taste

1 Heat a large saucepan over medium heat, add 2 tablespoons of the butter, sauté the mushrooms until they're browned, 3 to 4 minutes, remove, and reserve them.

2 Add the remaining butter to the saucepan, add the bell pepper, onion, jalapeño and cumin seed and sauté until they're soft, 3 to 5 minutes. Whisk in the flour, paprika and red pepper and mix well to eliminate any lumps that may form. Reduce the heat to low, stir in the chicken broth, and mix well. Add the half-and-half and cheese and stir continuously until the cheese has melted and the soup has thickened. Add the corn, parsley, pimiento and the reserved mushrooms; mix well and heat thoroughly. Salt to taste and serve immediately.

Serves 4 to 6   Preparation time: 20 mins   Cooking time: 20 mins

Green Chile Stew

This dish has been a popular staple in Santa Fe for hundreds of years, ever since the Spanish introduced domesticated pigs. Although it's a simple dish, the slow simmering blends the flavor of the pork so well with the chile that sometimes I make it with just pork and green chile.

$1^1/_2$ lbs (750 g) lean pork, cut into
$1^1/_2$-in (4-cm) cubes
$1^1/_2$ tablespoons oil
1 large onion, diced
2 cloves garlic, minced
4 cups (1 liter) pork or chicken broth
6 New Mexican green chiles, roasted
and peeled, sliced into thin strips to
yield about $1/_2$ cup
2 small tomatoes, peeled and
chopped
1 large potato, peeled and diced
$1/_2$ teaspoon dried oregano, preferably
Mexican
Salt to taste

1 In a heavy skillet, brown the pork over medium to medium-high heat, adding a little oil if needed. When the pork is browned, transfer it to a large stockpot.

2 Add 1 tablespoon of the oil to the same skillet and sauté the onion until golden brown, 2 to 3 minutes. Add the garlic and cook for an additional minute. Transfer the mixture to the pot with the pork.

3 Add the remaining ingredients to the stockpot and bring to just below boiling over high heat. Reduce the heat and simmer covered for 1 to $1^1/_2$ hours, or until the meat is very tender and starts to fall apart.

Note: For a meatless alternative, substitute pinto beans (which have been soaked overnight) and vegetable broth.

Serves 4   Preparation time: 20 mins   Cooking time: 1 hour 45 mins

Posole   Pork and Posole corn

Treating corn with lime to remove the tough skins was probably a technique the early Meso-American cultures passed on to the Pueblo Indians in New Mexico. The corn that is used is the same kind used to make hominy, but the processing imparts a different taste. This corn, called posole, is the main ingredient of this dish of the same name. It is traditionally served during the Christmas season, when a pot simmering on the stove provides welcoming fare for holiday well-wishers. Hominy corn can be substituted for the posole corn, although the taste will be different.

$3/4$ cup (125 g) dried posole
Water, enough to cover
1 lb (500 g) lean pork, cut into $1^1/_2$-in
    (4-cm) cubes
1 to 2 tablespoons oil
1 large onion, diced
2 cloves garlic, minced
2 cups (500 ml) pork or chicken broth
2 to 3 tablespoons ground New
    Mexican red chile
1 teaspoon dried oregano
Salt to taste
4 to 6 flour tortillas, to serve
$1/_2$ portion Chile Colorado (page 30)

Garnishes
Chopped fresh cilantro (coriander
    leaves)
Diced onions

1 In a large saucepan or stockpot, cover the posole with water and soak it overnight. Bring the water and posole to a boil, reduce the heat, and simmer until the kernels start to become tender, 1 to $1^1/_2$ hours. Add more water if necessary.

2 In a heavy skillet, brown the pork over medium-high heat, adding a little oil if needed. When the pork is browned, remove from the heat and add it to the posole.

3 In the same skillet over medium heat, sauté the onion with additional oil if needed, until it turns a golden brown, 2 to 3 minutes. Add the garlic and cook for an additional minute. Remove from the heat and transfer the mixture to the stockpot with the posole.

4 Add the pork or chicken broth, chile and oregano to the stockpot and salt to taste. Continue to cook over high heat until just below boiling, then reduce the heat and simmer for 1 to $1^1/_2$ hours, or until the meat is very tender and starts to fall apart. Add more broth or water if necessary. Remove from the heat.

5 Place the Garnishes in small serving bowls, ladle the stew into large soup bowls and serve immediately with warm flour tortillas and Chile Colorado.

Serves 4 to 6   Preparation time: 20 mins + time to prepare Chile Colorado + overnight soaking   Cooking time: 3 hours 15 mins

Dried Corn Stew   Chicos

Chicos are corn that has been steamed before drying. You will need to soak the chicos overnight for this recipe.

1 cup (250 g) dried chicos
Water, enough to cover
2 teaspoons oil
1 large onion, diced
1 clove garlic, minced
$1^1/_2$ teaspoons dried oregano,
    preferably Mexican
2 dried New Mexican red chile pods,
    crushed
Salt to taste
4 to 6 flour tortillas, to serve
$1/_2$ portion Chile Colorado (page 30),
    to serve

1 In a large saucepan or stockpot, cover the chicos with water and soak them overnight. Bring the water and chicos to a boil, reduce the heat, and cook until the kernels start to become tender, 1 to 2 hours. Add more water if necessary.

2 In a heavy skillet over medium heat, add the oil and onion, and sauté until golden brown, 2 to 3 minutes. Add the garlic and cook for another minute. Remove the mixture from the heat and transfer to the stockpot with the chicos.

3 Add the oregano to the stockpot and continue to cook for 1 hour, or until the chicos are tender. Add the crushed chile, salt to taste and simmer for 5 more minutes. Remove from the heat.

4 To serve, ladle the chicos into individual bowls and serve with warm flour tortillas and Chile Colorado.

Serves 4 to 6   Preparation time: 15 mins + time to prepare Chile Colorado + overnight soaking   Cooking time: 3 hours 10 mins

Preparing Chile Rellenos

Method

Step 1: Peel a roasted chile, then make a slit near the top and remove the seeds through it. Stuff it with the filling.

Step 2: Roll the chile in flour then shake off the excess flour.

Step 3: Dip the chile in the batter. Fry it in oil, turning it once so it browns on both sides. Drain on paper towels.

Chile rellenos literally means "stuffed chiles," and any chile that is large enough to stuff can be used. In Mexico the most common chile used is the poblano, but many others—jalapeños, dried anchos and chipotles—are also popular. In the Southwest, the green New Mexican is the chile of choice.

If you use fresh chiles, they need to be roasted, then peeled and deseeded (see pages 19 to 21), leaving the stem and the flesh intact. Dried chiles must be soaked and drained before stuffing.

Just as you can use any chile that can be stuffed, any filling that you can get into the chile will work. The simplest and most popular one is cheese, most commonly Cheddar, but any type of soft cheese is fine. Keep in mind that whatever filling you use needs to be firm enough to not leak out during cooking. Meat or fish must be precooked because the frying time is not long enough to cook the filling.

To fill the chile (see the recipe on page 54), make a slit near the top large enough for you to remove the seeds and put in the stuffing. Fill the chile but don't pack it too full; you want to be able to close the chile before dipping it in the flour and batter. If you need to, overlap the sides along the slit, holding them together with a toothpick. Just remember to remove the toothpick before serving.

Coat the chiles well with batter, as the coating prevents the chiles from absorbing oil. For frying, the oil must be hot enough so the coating will cook and brown quickly. If the chiles sit too long, they absorb too much oil and become soggy and greasy.

Slide the chiles, a couple at a time, into the hot oil. As they are browning, carefully spoon some of the hot oil on top to set the batter. Brown both sides, turning only once. Remove and drain the chiles. Serve hot with or without a sauce or salsa on top.

Making a Tamale

Method 1

Step 1: Soak the corn husks in water to soften them. Spread the masa dough on the husk and place the filling on top.

Step 2: Fold the husk around the masa and filling.

Step 3: Use two strips of leftover corn husks to tie the tamale at both ends.

Tamales are small corn husk packages that are filled with corn masa and lard or shortening. They are flavored with a wide variety of ingredients, including cheese, beans, chiles, beef, chicken and fish. They are typically steamed. Tamales freeze well and can be steamed to reheat them, so you may want to make them in large quantities.

Tamales can be tied two ways, both illustrated here. For these tamales, dried corn husks that have been soaked are used. In some Mexican versions, tender fresh corn husks are used.

Once they are folded, steam the tamales. They are ready when the filling is firm and pulls away from the corn husk easily.

Method 2

Step 1: To make a squarer tamale, soak the corn husks, then spread on the masa dough and filling.

Step 2: Fold up the husk and fold the tapered end over the filled husk.

Step 3: Fold the other end over the filled husk and tie it around the middle with a strip of corn husk.

Southwest Summer Vegetable Tamales

The name "tamale" comes from the Nahuatl Indian word *tamalli*, and it is one of the oldest Mexican foods. Traditionally, lard has been used as the fat in making tamales, but for the health-conscious, vegetable shortening may be substituted.

24 dried corn husks
4 cups (700 g) dried masa
$1/2$ teaspoon baking powder
1 teaspoon salt
$2^1/_2$ cups (625 ml) vegetable broth or
   water
$2/_3$ cup (150 ml) shortening
1 cup (125 g) grated Asadero or
   Monterey Jack cheese

Filling
2 cups (400 g) whole-kernel corn,
   fresh or frozen
1 large zucchini (courgette), diced
1 small onion, diced
4 tablespoons chopped New
   Mexican green or poblano chile,
   roasted, deseeded and peeled
1 teaspoon chopped fresh marjoram,
   or $1/_2$ teaspoon dried
1 cup (250 ml) Green Tomatillo
   Sauce (page 29)
Salt and freshly ground black pepper
   to taste

1 For the Filling, combine the corn, zucchini, onion, chile and marjoram in a large bowl. Add the Green Tomatillo Sauce and lightly mix the ingredients. Season with the salt and pepper and set the mixture aside.
2 Place the corn husks in a shallow pan, cover them with water, and soak them for 15 to 20 minutes to soften.
3 In another bowl, mix together the masa, baking powder and salt. Slowly add the broth until the mixture holds together. Whip or beat the shortening until it's fluffy. Add the masa mixture to the shortening and continue to beat until fluffy. Drop a teaspoonful of the masa dough into a glass of cold water: if it floats, it is ready. If it sinks, continue to beat it. Test until it floats.
4 To assemble, place a couple of tablespoons of the masa dough in the center of a large husk, or 2 smaller husks that overlap, and spread thinly. Place a couple of tablespoons of the Filling down the center of the dough and sprinkle on a little of the cheese. Fold the husks over and tie (see page 57).
5 Place a rack in the bottom of a steamer or large pot and add water to cover the bottom. Arrange the tamales either standing up or in layers, but do not pack them tightly, because they expand as they cook. Cover the tamales with a towel or additional corn husks. Steam them until cooked, 30 to 40 minutes. To test for doneness, open the end of one tamale—if the masa pulls away from the wrapper, the tamales are done. Allow them to cool slightly and serve with additional tomatillo sauce.

Makes 24 tamales   Preparation time: 1 hour   Cooking time: 40 mins

Venison Red Chile Stew

When you order "chili" in Santa Fe, you will be served a variation of this recipe, not a soupy bean dish. It is a recipe that has its roots in old Pueblo Indian cooking and is basically meat in a seasoned chile sauce. Pork and beef are more commonly used, but venison is a tasty variation.

6 to 8 dried New Mexican red chiles
1 ancho chile
1 pasilla chile (optional)
2 tablespoons oil
2 lbs (1 kg) venison, cut into $1^1/_2$-in
   (4-cm) cubes
1 large onion, chopped
3 cloves garlic, minced
3 cups (750 ml) beef broth
Salt to taste

Serves 4 to 6
Preparation time: 30 mins
Cooking time: 2 hours

1 Preheat the oven to 250°F (120°C, gas mark $1/_2$). Place the chiles on a baking pan and toast for 15 minutes, or until fragrant, being careful not to let them burn. Remove the stems and seeds from the chiles and crumble them into a bowl. Cover them with hot water and let them steep for 15 minutes, or until soft. Drain them and discard the water.
2 In a heavy skillet, heat the oil over medium heat, add the venison, and brown. Remove the meat and add the onion to the pan. Add more oil if necessary and sauté until the onion begins to brown, 2 to 3 minutes. Add the garlic and sauté for 1 to 2 more minutes.
3 Place the chiles, onion mixture and 1 cup (250 ml) of the beef broth in a blender or food processor. Purée until smooth, adding more broth if necessary. Strain the mixture through a sieve.
4 In a large saucepan, combine the venison, ground ingredients and remaining broth. Bring it to just below boiling, reduce the heat, and simmer until the meat is very tender and the sauce has thickened, 1 to $1^1/_2$ hours. Salt to the taste and remove from heat.

Roasted Poblano Chiles Stuffed with Quinoa, Mushrooms and Pine Nuts   Poblano Relleno

This is another chile relleno with a delicious mushroom, quinoa and goat cheese filling. Piñon trees grow extensively throughout northern New Mexico, and the nuts have been gathered and used in cooking for hundreds of years. The delicate yet nutty flavor of the quinoa (pronounced KEEN-wah) is enhanced by the addition of the nuts. See page 56 for information on stuffing a chile.

4 poblano chiles, roasted, peeled
  and deseeded, with stems left on

Filling
1 cup (175 g) quinoa
4 tablespoons sliced mushrooms,
  such as shiitake, portobello or crimini
2 shallots, sliced
1 clove garlic, minced
2 tablespoons butter or olive oil
1 teaspoon fresh thyme
$^1/_2$ teaspoon dried sage
$^1/_8$ to $^1/_4$ teaspoon ground chile de
  Árbol
1 cup (200 g) goat cheese
3 tablespoons New Mexican piñon
  nuts or regular pine nuts
Salt to taste

Fresh Red Chile Sauce
12 fresh New Mexican red chiles,
  roasted, peeled, stems and seeds
  removed
2 cloves garlic
$^1/_2$ teaspoon salt
$^1/_2$ teaspoon dried oregano, preferably
  Mexican
2 cups (500 ml) water

1 Prepare the Fresh Red Chile Sauce by placing all the ingredients in a blender or food processor and grinding until smooth, adding more water if necessary. Sometimes fresh chiles will still have fibers after they are puréed; strain if a smoother sauce is desired. Adjust the seasonings to taste, transfer to a bowl and set aside. This makes about $2^1/_2$ cups (625 ml) of sauce.
2 Preheat the oven to 350°F (180°C, gas mark 4).
3 To make the Filling, begin by rinsing the quinoa twice in a fine strainer. Place it in a saucepan and cover it with water (the water should be 1 in or $2^1/_2$ cm, above the surface of the grain). Bring to a boil, reduce the heat, and simmer until all the liquid has been absorbed, 15 to 20 minutes. Transfer the quinoa to a mixing bowl and fluff with a fork.
4 In a small skillet over medium heat, sauté the mushrooms, shallots and garlic in the butter until they've softened, about 5 minutes. Add the thyme, sage and chile and sauté for an additional minute. Remove the skillet from the heat and add its contents, along with the cheese and pine nuts, to the quinoa. Combine well and salt to taste.
5 Stuff the chiles with the Filling, place them on an oiled baking pan and warm them in the oven.
6 Place a *poblano relleno* on each plate, top it with the chile sauce and serve.

Serves 4   Preparation time: 45 mins   Cooking time: 45 mins

Grilled Steaks with Chimayó, Chile and Cumin
Carne Asada

Carne asada means "grilled meat," and this dish is very similar to those *asadas* served in Mexico. Quick and easy to prepare, these steaks are usually served with a tomato-based salsa, such as Pico de Gallo, that complements the hearty beef flavor.

Literally translated as "rooster beak," Pico de Gallo salsa goes by a number of other names—salsa fresca, salsa fria, salsa cruda and salsa Mexicana. Whatever it's called, it is a wonderful salsa that you can serve with chips or as an accompaniment to a number of dishes. The secret to a good Pico de Gallo is in the texture. The ingredients should be finely chopped but not minced.

3 fresh limes
4 ribeye steaks (350 g in total)
5 cloves garlic, chopped
1 tablespoon ground red Chimayó chile
1 teaspoon freshly ground black pepper
1 teaspoon ground cumin
$^1/_4$ cup (60 ml) olive oil
8 corn tortillas, to serve

Pico de Gallo Salsa
2 medium-sized tomatoes, finely chopped
1 medium-sized red onion, finely chopped
2 jalapeño chiles, finely chopped
2 cloves garlic, minced
4 tablespoons chopped cilantro (coriander leaves)
3 tablespoons oil
3 tablespoons red wine vinegar
Salt to taste

1 Prepare the Pica de Gallo Salsa by combining all the ingredients in a bowl and mixing thoroughly. Let the salsa sit at room temperature for at least an hour before serving. This makes about 2 cups (500 ml) of salsa.
2 Cut the limes in half and squeeze the juice over both sides of the steaks. Rub the garlic on the steaks; sprinkle the chile, pepper and cumin over the steaks; and marinate them for 30 minutes at room temperature.
3 Prepare a charcoal grill. When the coals are medium hot, brush the steaks with oil and grill them to the desired doneness. Immediately serve the steaks, accompanied with the salsa and warm corn tortillas.

Note: The key to proper preparation of salsa is never to use a food processor or blender—all ingredients should be cut by hand to ensure a nice texture.

Serves 2 to 4   Preparation time: 30 mins + 1 hour to marinate
Cooking time: 15 mins

Steak Dunigan   Rosalea Murphy, The Pink Adobe Restaurant

This dish was named after its inventor, Pat Dunigan, who insisted on adding green chiles to his steak whenever he ate at the restaurant. Soon there was such a demand for a steak with chiles that Rosalea had to put it on the menu. It has become a signature dish of the Pink.

4 large fresh mushrooms, thinly
  sliced
4 tablespoons butter ($^1/_2$ stick)
Hickory-smoked salt or regular salt
2 top-grade New York sirloin steaks
  (about 1 lb/500 g in total)

Green Chile and Onion Sauce
2 tablespoons olive oil
1 medium-sized onion, minced
2 cans (each 4 oz/125 g) New
  Mexican green chiles, drained and
  chopped
$^1/_4$ teaspoon dried oregano
$^1/_4$ teaspoon salt
1 teaspoon Tabasco sauce or
  chopped jalapeño chile

1 Prepare the Green Chile and Onion Sauce by heating the oil in a saucepan over medium-high heat and sauté the onion until it's soft and translucent, 2 to 3 minutes. Add the remaining sauce ingredients, reduce the heat, and simmer for an additional 5 minutes. Keep the sauce warm in a 200°F (100°C, gas mark $^1/_4$) oven.

2 In another pan over medium heat, sauté the mushrooms in the butter until they're soft, approximately 5 minutes. Remove the pan from the heat and also keep it warm in the oven.

3 Shake the hickory salt on both sides of the steaks. Broil or grill to the desired doneness (10 to 15 minutes for rare; 15 to 20 minutes for medium), turning them once.

4 Transfer the steaks to individual plates and divide the mushrooms over them. Cover each with the Green Chile and Onion Sauce and serve at once.

Serves 2   Preparation time: 10 mins   Cooking time: 40 mins

Carne Adovada   Al Lucero, Maria's New Mexican Kitchen

This simple to prepare but very tasty dish evolved from the need to preserve meat without refrigeration. Since chile acts as an antioxidant, covering or marinating pork in a chile sauce kept the meat from spoiling before the advent of the icebox. One of the most popular dishes in New Mexico, *carne adovada* is on the menu for breakfast, lunch and dinner.

2 lbs (1 kg) pork butt (round), fat trimmed and cut into 1-in (2½-cm) cubes
1 cup (200 g) crushed New Mexican red chile, seeds included
1 tablespoon garlic powder
1 teaspoon salt
6 flour tortillas, to serve
1 portion Pico de Gallo Salsa (page 63), to serve

Red Chile Sauce
6 to 8 dried New Mexican red chile pods
4 cloves garlic
½ teaspoon salt
3 cups (750 ml) water

1 Preheat the oven to 375°F (190°C, gas mark 5).
2 Place the meat in a lightly oiled or sprayed deep baking pan and bake it for 30 minutes, stirring often to ensure even cooking.
3 To make the Red Chile Sauce, place the chiles in a medium-sized saucepan and cover them with hot water. Steep until they're soft, about 20 minutes. Drain them and discard the water. Place the softened chile pods, garlic, salt, and water into a blender or food processor and purée the mixture until it's smooth, adding additional water if necessary. Pour the mixture into the saucepan and simmer until it thickens slightly. Remove from the heat.
4 Remove the baking pan with the meat from the oven but do not pour off the juices. Stir in the Red Chile Sauce, the crushed chile, garlic powder and salt. Return it to the oven and bake, stirring occasionally, until the pork is tender enough to cut with a fork, 30 to 45 minutes. Serve with the flour tortillas, accompanied by the Pico de Gallo Salsa.

Serves 6   Preparation time: 30 mins   Cooking time: 1 hour 15 mins

Rack of Lamb with Heirloom Bean Ragout

Jeff Copeland, Santacafé

The lamb for this dish should be "frenched", that is, the meat should be cut away to expose the end of the bone, as in the photo. It's easiest to have a butcher do this. This dish uses three heirloom beans, but any three-bean combination will taste good. Try substituting black-eyed peas, white northern or even pinto beans; you can also use canned beans to reduce the cooking time. Pomegranate molasses, which can be found in most import or Indian markets, makes a nice glaze for the lamb.

$1/4$ cup (45 g) dried Anasazi beans
$1/4$ cup (45 g) dried palomino beans
$1/4$ cup (45 g) dried rattlesnake beans
5 tablespoons unsalted butter
1 medium-sized yellow onion, cut into thin strips
1 medium-sized red onion, cut into thin strips
1 tablespoon chopped garlic
2 cups (500 ml) veal demiglace or chicken stock
4 frenched racks of lamb (12 oz/350 g in total)
Salt and freshly ground black pepper to taste
Olive oil
1 cup (250 ml) pomegranate molasses
1 cup (50 g) lightly chopped fresh herbs such as thyme, rosemary,
   sage or marjoram

1 Place each of the beans in separate bowls, cover them with water, and refrigerate them overnight.
2 In separate saucepans, cook the beans until they're tender, 1 to 2 hours. It is important to keep them separate because they have different cooking times. Drain the beans and keep them warm.
3 Preheat a grill or oven to 400°F (200°C, gas mark 6), or a broiler, depending on how you want to cook the lamb. If you choose to use an oven, be sure to also preheat the pan you will use to cook your lamb.
4 Heat 2 tablespoons of the butter in a large skillet or sauté pan over medium heat. When the butter starts to bubble, add the onion and sauté until it's transparent. Add the garlic and all the beans and toss them in the skillet. Add the demiglace or chicken stock and simmer to reduce the sauce until it coats the back of a spoon. Remove from the heat.
5 Generously season the lamb with salt, pepper and a touch of the oil. Place it on the preheated cooking surface and cook to an internal temperature of 122°F (50°C). Remove and allow the meat to rest at room temperature, but not longer than 8 minutes. Coat the lamb with the molasses, allowing a crust to form.
6 Stir the remaining butter into the bean mixture to thicken the sauce. Add the fresh herbs and season with the salt and pepper to taste.
7 Pile the beans in the center of a plate. Cut the lamb into chops and place them decoratively around the beans and serve immediately.

Note: Pomegranate molasses is available in Middle Eastern food stores, or you can make your own by following the recipe on page 26.

Serves 4   Preparation time: 30 mins + overnight soaking
Cooking time: 2 hours 30 mins

Orange-marinated Chicken Fajitas Sante Fe School of Cooking

Fajitas means "little belts"; traditionally they have been made with marinated and grilled skirt steak. Mexican-American cowboys are credited with creating the dish as a way of using tough, inexpensive cuts of meat. At the Santa Fe School of Cooking they serve this dish with Spanish Rice (page 91), Santa Fe Coleslaw and Pickled Red Onions (page 31) as accompaniments.

6 skinless, boneless chicken breasts (about 5 oz/150 g each), trimmed of all fat and pounded to a thickness of $1/2$ in (1 cm)
$1/2$ teaspoon salt
6 flour tortillas, to serve

Orange Marinade
3 large seedless oranges, unpeeled, cut into eighths
1 medium-sized onion, cut into eighths
$1/2$ can (100 ml) *chipotles en adobo* sauce
3 cloves garlic
$1/3$ cup (25 g) coarsely chopped fresh cilantro (coriander leaves)
4 sprigs fresh rosemary, leaves only, or 2 teaspoons dried
4 sprigs fresh thyme, leaves only, or 1 teaspoon dried
4 sprigs fresh marjoram or oregano, leaves only, or 2 teaspoons dried
1 teaspoon kosher salt plus additional as needed

1 Place the Orange Marinade ingredients in a food processor and pulse until thoroughly combined, but forms a rather coarse purée.
2 Layer the chicken breasts in a non-reactive dish and spread the Orange Marinade over them. Marinate the chicken in the refrigerator for 12 to 24 hours. Clean the marinade from the chicken and season with the salt.
3 Lightly oil a cast-iron grill pan using a paper towel and heat over high heat until a drop of water sizzles upon contact, about 3 minutes. Reduce the heat to medium-high, and cook the marinated chicken breasts until they're browned on one side 3 to 5 minutes. Rotate the chicken 45 degrees about halfway through cooking to create crisscross grill marks. Turn over the breasts and cook until they are browned on both sides and done throughout but still juicy, 4 to 5 minutes.
4 Slice the chicken breasts into strips and serve with the flour tortillas, Spanish Rice (page 91), Santa Fe Coleslaw (see below) and Pickled Red Onions (page 31).

Serves 6   Preparation time: 30 mins + overnight to marinate
Cooking time: 10 mins

Santa Fe Coleslaw Sante Fe School of Cooking

1 lb (500 g) green cabbage, sliced into thin strips
1 medium-sized cucumber, peeled, deseeded and thinly sliced diagonally
5 scallions (spring onions), thinly sliced diagonally
1 medium-sized red and 1 medium-sized yellow bell pepper (capsicum), cut into strips
2 celery ribs, thinly sliced diagonally
1 large carrot, shredded
1 small white onion, cut in thin slivers (optional)

Dressing
4 tablespoons freshly squeezed lime juice
2 tablespoons cider vinegar
2 teaspoons hot pepper sauce
$1/4$ cup (50 g) sugar
1 teaspoon salt

1 Combine all the vegetables in a large mixing bowl.
2 Combine the Dressing ingredients in a small bowl and stir until the sugar has dissolved.
3 Pour the Dressing over the vegetables and toss well. Let the mixture stand at room temperature for at least 30 minutes, tossing often, before serving. For maximum color and flavor, serve within 3 to 4 hours.

Serves 6   Preparation time: 30 mins + 30 mins to develop flavor

Tacos and Tostadas

A taco is a stuffed corn tortilla, which can be served either soft or crisp; a tostada is the flat version of a crisp taco. As with many tortilla-based dishes, the fillings are used interchangeably, and the types of fillings are limited only by your imagination. This recipe can be made either with Chicken Enchiladas (page 75) or Beef Filling.

12 taco or tostada shells (page 31)
3 to 4 romaine lettuce leaves, sliced into thin strips
1 large tomato, finely diced
1 cup (125 g) grated Monterey Jack cheese
1 cup (125 g) grated Cheddar cheese
Guacamole (page 32) (optional)
Sour cream (optional)
1 portion Chile Piquín Salsa (page 29) or New Mexican Green Chile Salsa (page 31), to serve

Beef Filling
2 lbs (1 kg) beef chuck roast, cut into small pieces
2 cups (500 ml) beef broth, or enough to cover the beef
2 pasilla chiles, stems removed, torn into pieces
1 dried New Mexican red chile, stem and seeds removed, torn into pieces
1 small onion, coarsely chopped
2 cloves garlic, chopped
1 teaspoon dried oregano, preferably Mexican
$1/4$ teaspoon ground cumin
Salt to taste

Refried Beans
1 tablespoon oil
2 cups (350 g) cooked pinto beans
1 cup (250 ml) bean liquid or water
1 tablespoon ground New Mexican red chile
$1/4$ teaspoon minced garlic
Pinch of ground cumin
Salt to taste

1 Prepare the Beef Filling by covering the beef with water or broth in a large pot and add the chiles, onion and garlic. Bring it to a boil, reduce the heat, cover and simmer until the meat is tender and starts to fall apart, about 1 hour. Allow the meat to cool in the broth. Remove the meat from the broth and discard any fatty pieces. Using two forks or your fingers, shred the meat. Season the beef with the oregano, cumin and salt. Alternatively, prepare the Chicken Enchilada Filling by following the recipe on page 75.
2 To make the Refried Beans, heat the oil in a skillet over medium heat. Add the beans and the liquid and mash the beans to the desired consistency; they may all be smooth, or some beans may be left whole. Reduce the heat, stir in the chile, garlic and cumin, and simmer for 10 minutes, adding additional liquid if needed. Salt to taste.
3 To assemble, place the filling on the bottom of either a taco or a tostada shell, and then layer the remaining ingredients—lettuce, tomato and cheese—over the filling. Spoon Guacamole and sour cream on top of the tacos or tostadas if desired. Serve with the salsa on the side.

Makes 12   Preparation time: 30 mins   Cooking time: 1 hour 15 mins

Red Corn Rubbed Chicken   Flynt Payne, Inn of the Anasazi

At the Inn of the Anasazi they serve this chicken with a tangy Apple Poblano Slaw.

2 red corn tortillas
5 ancho chiles, sliced into strips
15 fresh cilantro (coriander) leaves
4 tablespoons flour
Pinch of salt
Pinch of freshly ground black pepper
2 chicken breasts, bone attached
1 egg, beaten
2 tablespoons oil

Habanero-lime Molasses
1 cup (250 ml) molasses
Juice and zest of 1 lime
1 habanero chile, minced

Apple Poblano Slaw
1 Granny Smith apple, sliced into thin
  strips
$1/2$ jicama, sliced into thin strips
1 red bell pepper (capsicum), sliced
  into thin strips
1 poblano chile, sliced into thin strips
Juice and zest of 1 lime
Zest of 1 lemon
1 tablespoon olive oil
1 tablespoon gold tequila
1 teaspoon brown sugar
Kosher salt and freshly ground black
  pepper to taste
4 fresh mint leaves

1 To make the Habanero-lime Molasses, combine all the ingredients in a large saucepan. Bring the mixture to a simmer and cook it over low heat for 15 minutes, stirring often to prevent burning. Allow it to cool, then strain.
2 Preheat the oven to 350°F (180°C, gas mark 4).
3 Cut the tortillas into long, thin strips and place them in a bowl. Add the chile strips to the tortillas along with the cilantro leaves. Place the egg in a separate bowl.
4 Season the flour with salt and pepper and place it in another bowl. Dredge the chicken with the flour and dip it in the egg, then in the tortilla mix. Coat the chicken well and set it aside.
5 To make the Apple Poblano Slaw, combine the apple, jicama, bell pepper and chile strips in a large bowl. Add the lime juice and zest as well as the lemon zest, and toss. Combine the oil, tequila and sugar in a separate bowl and mix them well. Add this to the slaw, tossing to combine. Season with the salt and pepper. Mix well and garnish with the mint leaves.
6 Heat the oil in a sauté pan over medium heat. Sauté the chicken in the pan until the tortilla strips are lightly browned, then remove the chicken. Finish the chicken in the oven for 15 minutes, or until the juices run clear when the meat is pricked.
7 Place the chicken on individual plates and top each with the slaw. Drizzle the Habanero-lime Molasses over the entire plate.

Serves 2   Preparation time: 45 mins   Cooking time: 45 mins

Blue Corn Stacked Chicken Enchiladas

The name "enchilada" refers to a dish of rolled or flat tortillas, usually corn, stuffed with a filling and topped with a chile sauce. These enchiladas can be either served whole as a main dish or cut into wedges and served as a side dish.

Oil, for frying
12 blue corn tortillas
1 portion either Chili Colorado (page 30) or Green Chile Sauce (page 30)
2 cups (250 g) shredded Monterey Jack cheese
1 small onion, thinly sliced
4 tablespoons chopped fresh cilantro (coriander leaves)
Shredded lettuce, to garnish
Chopped tomatoes, to garnish

Chicken Enchilada Filling
2 boneless chicken breasts, skin removed
2 tablespoons oil
1 medium-sized onion, chopped
2 cloves garlic, minced
1 jalapeño chile, chopped
$1/2$ teaspoon ground cumin
$1/2$ teaspoon dried oregano, preferably Mexican
2 cups (500 ml) water or chicken broth

1 To prepare the Chicken Enchilada Filling, cut the chicken into large pieces. Heat the oil in a heavy skillet over medium-high heat, add the chicken, onion and garlic and sauté until soft, 2 to 3 minutes. Add the jalapeño, cumin, oregano and broth; cover the skillet and simmer until the chicken is very tender and starts to fall apart, about 30 minutes. Remove from the heat and allow the chicken to cool in the broth for 10 minutes. Remove the chicken. Using a couple of forks or your fingers, shred the chicken.

2 Preheat the oven to 300°F (150°C, gas mark 2).

3 Pour the oil into a skillet to a depth of 1 in (2$1/2$ cm) and heat it over high heat until very hot. Make a small slit in the center of each tortilla to prevent it from puffing up during frying. Fry the tortillas for a couple of seconds on each side to soften, being careful they do not become too crisp. Remove the tortillas and drain on paper towels.

4 To assemble the enchiladas, pour a small amount of the sauce of your choice on the bottom of a casserole dish, place a tortilla on top, then some chicken shreds, cheese, onion, cilantro and then more sauce. Repeat the procedure for an additional layer if desired and finish with a tortilla. Repeat with the remaining tortillas and filling.

5 Bake the enchiladas in the oven for 5 to 10 minutes, or until they're thoroughly heated. To serve, garnish with the lettuce, tomatoes, more shredded cheese, additional tortillas if desired and pour additional sauce over the top.

Serves 4 to 6   Preparation time: 30 mins   Cooking time: 45 mins

Chipotle Beef and Bean Burritos

Burritos, or "little burros," are flour tortillas that are wrapped or folded around a filling. This is one of the most common uses of flour tortillas. Any of the fillings for tacos can be used, and burritos may be smothered in a chile sauce or folded up and eaten as a sandwich. Breakfast burritos filled with scrambled eggs, potatoes, bacon, sausage (or chorizo) and served with a chile sauce are one of our most popular "fast foods."

4 flour tortillas
$1/2$ portion Chipotle Sauce (page 30)
2 cups (500 ml) Refried Beans (page 71)
1 cup (200 g) Beef Filling (page 71)
1 cup (125 g) grated Cheddar cheese

1 Soften the tortillas by wrapping them in a cloth towel and heating them in the microwave for 20 seconds on high or by placing them on a hot comal for a minute or two.

2 To assemble the burritos, lay the tortilla on a flat surface and ladle on some of the sauce, spread a layer of beans over the sauce, and top with some beef and cheese. Fold up one end of the tortilla about 1 in (2$1/2$ cm) over the filling. Next, fold the right and left sides over the folded end, overlapping one of the sides, and finally fold down the remaining end. Serve with or without additional sauce over the top.

Makes 4   Preparation time: 30 mins   Cooking time: 2 mins + time to cook Refried Beans and Beef Filling

Pollo Pibil   Katharine Kagel, Cafe Pasqual's

This spiced chicken dish came to Santa Fe by way of the Yucatán. The *pibil* method of cooking involves wrapping the meat in banana leaves, burying it in a pit, and roasting it slowly. This recipe employs a grill to achieve the same results. The achiote, a paste of dried annatto seeds, is a sweet, earthy counterpoint to the citrus and garlic flavors. Be sure to allow plenty of time for marinating the chicken well; 24 hours is best. At Cafe Pasqual's they serve this dish with Saffron Rice (page 28) and grilled vegetables.

6 skinless, boneless chicken breasts, halved
6 grilled scallions (spring onions)
6 large pieces banana leaf

Marinade
4 teaspoons cumin seeds
1 cinnamon stick, 3 in (8 cm) long, preferably Mexican
1 teaspoon whole cloves
1 1/2 tablespoons whole black peppercorns
1/2 cup (125 ml) achiote paste
3 teaspoons kosher salt
2 tablespoons minced garlic
2 cups (500 ml) freshly squeezed orange juice
1/2 cup (125 ml) freshly squeezed lime juice
2 tablespoons fresh marjoram leaves, or 1 tablespoon dried
1/2 cup (125 ml) olive oil

1 To prepare the Marinade, roast the cumin, cinnamon, cloves and peppercorns in a small, dry sauté pan over medium heat, shaking the pan frequently, until fragrant, about 2 minutes. Remove the spices from the heat and allow them to cool. Place the spices in a spice mill, coffee grinder or mortar and grind them until they're pulverized. Place the spices, achiote paste, salt, garlic, orange and lime juices, marjoram and oil in a blender or food processor and process just long enough to blend.

2 In a shallow non-reactive dish, pour the Marinade evenly over the top of the chicken breasts to cover them completely. Cover the dish and let the chicken breasts marinate in the refrigerator for at least 24 hours (up to 36 hours), turning them frequently.

3 Place the marinated chicken, skin-side down, on a charcoal grill about 6 in (15 cm) above the coals, and grill over medium-hot, basting with the Marinade and turning once, until they're done, 15 to 20 minutes' total grilling time. Be careful not to overcook them; the chicken should be juicy.

4 Garnish each cooked breast with one grilled scallion and serve on a banana leaf.

Serves 6   Preparation time: 20 mins + 24 hours to marinate
Cooking time: 25 mins

Fire-roasted Vegetables   Katharine Kagel, Cafe Pasqual's

1 large red onion, sliced into thick rings
2 red bell peppers (capsicum), deseeded and cut into long strips 1/2 in (1 cm) wide
2 yellow squash, sliced lengthwise into 1/4-in (1/2-cm) wide pieces
2 zucchini (courgettes), sliced lengthwise into 1/4-in (1/2-cm) wide pieces
2 Japanese eggplants (aubergines), sliced lengthwise into 1/4-in (1/2-cm) wide pieces

Marinade
1 cup (250 ml) olive oil
1/3 cup (90 ml) balsamic vinegar
1 tablespoon minced garlic
1 teaspoon kosher salt
2 teaspoons freshly ground black pepper

1 Prepare the Marinade for the vegetables by combining the olive oil, vinegar, garlic, salt and pepper in a bowl, and mixing well.

2 Place all the vegetables in a shallow non-reactive bowl and pour the Marinade over the top, coating each piece well. Marinate at room temperature for 4 to 6 hours.

3 Grill the marinated vegetables on a charcoal grill over medium-hot, basting with the Marinade and turning frequently, until they're charred, 7 to 12 minutes.

Serves 6   Preparation time: 20 mins + 6 hours to marinate   Cooking time: 15 mins

Chilean Sea Bass Napoleon   Kelly Rogers, La Casa Sena

Kelly Rogers serves this layered dish over sautéed chayote squash.

1 cup (100 g) shelled pistachios
8 pieces of Chilean sea bass fillet
   (about 2 oz/60 g each)
1 tablespoon olive oil
Pinch of salt and freshly ground black
   pepper
Fried tortilla triangles, to serve
Assorted greens (arugula, mâche, or
   romaine), to serve
Tangerine zest, to garnish

Tangerine Hot and Sour Sauce
1 teaspoon oil
1 jalapeño chile, chopped
1 tablespoon chopped fresh ginger
$2^{1}/_{2}$ teaspoons chopped garlic
2 cups (500 ml) tangerine juice
$^{1}/_{2}$ cup (100 g) sugar
$^{1}/_{2}$ cup (125 ml) white wine
$^{1}/_{2}$ teaspoon salt
1 tablespoon cornstarch mixed with
   3 tablespoons water

Charred Tomatillo Aïoli
6 tomatillos, husks removed
4 cloves garlic
2 slices red onion
1 tablespoon olive oil
Pinch of salt and freshly ground black
   pepper
Freshly squeezed juice of 1 lime
1 cup (250 ml) mayonnaise

1 Prepare the Tangerine Hot and Sour Sauce by heating the oil in a saucepan and sautéing the jalapeño, ginger and garlic until lightly browned. Add the tangerine juice, sugar, wine and salt, and simmer to reduce the sauce by half. Remove the pan from the heat, strain the sauce, and return it to the stove. Simmer the sauce and slowly add the cornstarch mixture to thicken it.

2 To make the Charred Tomatillo Aïoli, lightly toss the tomatillos, garlic and onion in the oil with a pinch of salt and pepper in a bowl. Grill the vegetables, or roast them in an oven, until they are blackened. Allow them to cool and place them in a blender or food processor with the lime juice and purée until smooth. Fold in the mayonnaise.

3 Preheat the oven to 250°F (120°C, gas mark $^{1}/_{2}$). Roast the pistachios until lightly browned, about 10 minutes. Let them cool, then chop the pistachios in a food mill or with a knife until fine.

4 Brush the fish with a little olive oil, season with the salt and pepper, and roll in the crushed pistachios. Grill the fish over medium-high heat for about 2 minutes, turning the fish often so that the pistachios do not burn. The fish should be firm when done.

5 Build the Napoleon on each of 4 plates by alternating a fried tortilla triangle, Charred Tomatillo Aïoli, greens and fish. Repeat this procedure and top the fish and the plate with the Tangerine Hot and Sour Sauce. Garnish with tangerine zest and serve immediately.

Serves 4   Preparation time: 45 mins   Cooking time: 45 mins

Trout in Adobe   Kelly Rogers, La Casa Sena

The "adobe" in this recipe is a low-fire clay that can be found in an art or ceramics supply store. The trick to serving this dish is to take two large spoons and gently tap the baked clay to crack and break it, rather like using drumsticks, not like using an ax to split wood. It is very important to be certain that the clay you are using is non-toxic; many clays contain lead, which could contaminate the food.

8 to 12 corn husks, soaked in water to soften
8 oz (250 g) butter (2 sticks), softened
2 cups (200 g) sliced mushrooms
1 tablespoon minced garlic
$^1/_2$ cup (125 ml) white wine
Salt to taste
5 lbs ($2^1/_2$ kg) potter's clay, divided into $1^1/_4$-lb (625-g) slabs
4 whole trout, filleted, with skin and head removed (8 pieces)
Assorted greens (arugula, romaine or mixed baby greens), to serve
Lemon wedges, to garnish

1 Preheat the oven to 400°F (200°C, gas mark 6).
2 Melt a couple of tablespoons of the butter in a sauté pan, add the mushrooms and garlic and sauté until they're soft. Raise the heat, add the wine, season with the salt, and let the mixture cool slightly. Fold in the remaining butter and let the sauce cool until it's firm and malleable.
3 Using a rolling pin, roll out the clay until it is about 12 x 18 in (30 x 45 cm) and $^1/_2$ in (1 cm) thick.
4 Place one quarter of the firm butter mixture between 2 of the trout fillets. Repeat this step with the other 6 fillets. Wrap each fillet sandwich in 2 or 3 corn husks so that it is completely covered. With the clay in front of you lengthwise, place the "tamale" on one side and fold over the clay. Cut out a fish shape and seal the clay with a fork around all edges. Cut vents in the sides to let air escape during cooking.
5 Place the "fish" either on a baking sheet or directly on the oven rack and bake for 15 to 20 minutes. The clay will get pale, dry and hard when it's done.
6 To serve, crack the clay with a large metal spoon and carefully push the clay off the "tamale." Take the "tamale" out and unfold the husks to expose the baked fish. Place it on a bed of prepared greens and garnish with lemon wedges.

Serves 4   Preparation time: 1 hour   Cooking time: 25 mins

Greens with Beans and Chile   Quelites

The word *quelite* is derived from the Nahuatl word *quilitl*, which the Indians in ancient Mexico used to describe any edible leafy green or herb.

1$^1/_2$ lbs (750 g) spinach
$^1/_2$ small white onion, sliced and separated into rings
1 tablespoon oil
2 cloves garlic (optional)
$^1/_2$ cup (40 g) cooked pinto beans
1 tablespoon crushed New Mexican red chile, seeds included
1 teaspoon distilled vinegar
Salt to taste

1 Rinse the spinach in a lot of water several times to remove any grit. Drain off the excess water and tear the leaves into smaller pieces if necessary, and place them in a bowl.
2 In a sauté pan over medium-high heat, quickly sauté the onion in the oil until they soften, 1 to 2 minutes. Remove from the heat.
3 Prepare a steamer and place the garlic, if desired, in the water at the bottom. Toss the spinach with a little oil and steam it until it's just soft, about 2 minutes.
4 Toss the cooked spinach with the onion, beans, chile and vinegar. Season to taste with the salt and serve immediately.

Serves 4   Preparation time: 15 mins   Cooking time: 5 mins

Drunken Beans   Beans Borracho

Borracho (which means "drunk") refers to the beer used to flavor the beans. Cooking the beans with garlic or epazote is said to help in digesting them. A little tequila can be substituted for the beer.

1$^1/_2$ cups (180 g) dried bolita or pinto beans
2 slices bacon, chopped (optional)
1 large onion, cut in thin wedges
2 cloves garlic
4 fresh epazote leaves, or 1 teaspoon dried
1 can (12 oz/350 ml) beer
2 small tomatoes, peeled and chopped
2 jalapeño chiles, cut into thin slices
Salt to taste

1 Cover the beans with water and discard any that float to the surface. Soak the beans overnight. Drain and rinse the beans.
2 In a small skillet, fry the bacon until it's just crisp, then remove and drain. Add the onion to the pan and sauté until it's soft, 2 to 3 minutes.
3 In a large pot, add the beans, water to cover, garlic and epazote. Bring the mixture to a boil, reduce the heat to medium-low, and simmer for 2 hours, or until the beans are tender. Add more water if needed or drain off some of the bean water if the mixture is too soupy. Add all the remaining ingredients, adjust the seasonings to taste and simmer for 20 to 30 more minutes.

Serves 4 to 6   Preparation time: 15 mins + overnight soaking
Cooking time: 2 hours 30 mins

Chipotle Crema Morel Stew   Katharine Kagel, Cafe Pasqual's

The baked acorn squash makes an elegant serving dish for this tasty stew.

4 acorn squash, tops cut off but stems kept attached, seeds and strings removed and reserved for the stock

Vegetable Stock
2 tablespoons olive oil
2 cloves garlic, coarsely chopped
1/2 bunch celery, leaves roughly chopped
Potato peelings from 3 to 4 small red potatoes
2 small onions, unpeeled and quartered
Reserved seeds and strings from squash
1 1/2 cups (375 ml) water

Stew
1/2 cup (125 ml) olive oil
1/2 cup (50 g) carrots, diced
1/2 cup (90 g) rutabaga, diced
1/4 cup (40 g) celery rib, cut into 1/2-in (1-cm) slices
3/4 cup (120 g) zucchini (courgette) or any summer squash, diced
3 to 4 small red potatoes (about 5 oz/150 g in total), diced
1 portobello mushroom, gills removed, thinly sliced
4 tablespoons fresh or rehydrated dried morels, quartered
1 clove garlic, minced
1 teaspoon grated fresh ginger
1 1/2 cups (375 ml) heavy (double) cream
2 teaspoons puréed *chipotles en adobo* sauce

1 Preheat the oven to 300°F (150°C, gas mark 2). Place the squash on a baking sheet, fill them with water and place their tops back on. Bake for 1 hour or until they're fork-tender.
2 In a stockpot, sauté all the Vegetable Stock ingredients in the oil over medium heat until they're lightly browned. Add 2 1/2 cups (625 ml) of water and bring the mixture to a rolling boil. Skim off and discard any foam that forms. Reduce the heat and simmer the stock uncovered for 1 hour. Strain the stock, discard the vegetables and reserve the stock.
3 In a large saucepan over medium heat, sauté all the Stew ingredients except the cream and *chipotles en adobo* sauce for 10 minutes. Add the reserved stock and simmer for 10 more minutes, or until the vegetables are fork-tender. Remove from the heat.
4 In another saucepan, simmer the cream until it's reduced by half. Add the *chipotles en adobo* sauce to the cream and stir until they're combined. Pour the mixture over the Stew and gently mix in until well incorporated.
5 To serve, fill the baked squash with the Stew and place the tops back on. Present the squash with garlic toast or other toasted bread.

Note: To rehydrate dried morels, soak them in enough hot water to cover for about 20 minutes. For a rich vegetable stock, add the soaking liquid to the simmering stock ingredients.

Serves 4   Preparation time: 45 mins   Cooking time: 2 hours

Potatoes with Red Chile   Papas Con Chile Colorado

The word "colorado" in the title refers to the red color of the chile. These potatoes are commonly served in place of hash browns at breakfast as well as at lunch and dinner. They are especially tasty when made with new potatoes because of their creamy texture and taste. Substitute chopped New Mexican green chile for a totally different taste.

$^1/_2$ cup (75 g) chopped onion
2 cloves garlic, minced
2 tablespoons oil
2 tablespoons crushed New Mexican
  red chile, seeds included
2 large potatoes, peeled and diced

1 Preheat the oven to 350°F (180°C, gas mark 4).
2 In a medium-sized skillet over medium heat, sauté the onion and garlic in the oil until they soften and start to brown. Remove from the heat and add the chile.
3 Toss the potatoes with the onion mixture until they're well coated and place them in a baking pan. Bake the potatoes for 40 minutes, or until they are tender.

Serves 4   Preparation time: 10 mins   Cooking time: 45 mins

Squash and Corn with Green Chile   Calabacitas

For hundreds of years squash and corn have been the staples of the Pueblo Indians in northern New Mexico, and these vegetables are combined with chile in this popular dish. The delicate flavors of the corn and squash in combination with the bite of the chile acts as a basis for variations. Use different types of summer squash, add cheese (such as Cheddar, Monterey Jack or Feta) or include chicken to turn this recipe from a side dish into an entrée.

2 tablespoons oil, preferably olive oil
2 zucchini squash (courgette), sliced
$^1/_2$ small white onion, sliced and
  separated into rings
2 cups (400 g) whole-kernel corn,
  fresh, frozen or canned
$^1/_2$ cup (100 g) chopped New
  Mexican green chiles (about 4 to 5),
  roasted, peeled and deseeded
2 teaspoons dried oregano
$^1/_2$ cup (125 ml) heavy cream
Salt to taste

In a sauté pan, heat the oil over medium heat and sauté the squash and onion for a couple of minutes. The squash should be tender but not soft. Add the corn, chile and oregano to the pan and sauté for 2 minutes. Stir in the cream, add salt to taste, and simmer for 3 to 4 minutes to blend the flavors.

Serves 4   Preparation time: 20 mins   Cooking time: 10 mins

Ramp Tart   Jeff Copeland, Santacafé

Ramps are wild onions that grow in deciduous forests in the spring. They have a long green shaft that is leafy at the top and crimson near the bulb. If picked while young, the whole plant is edible; otherwise only the bulb can be used. Most specialty food stores have ramps in the spring; but if they're not available, substitute scallions.

Tart Shell
$3^1/_2$ cups (500 g) flour
Pinch of salt
$1^1/_4$ cups (300 g) unsalted butter
3 egg yolks
$^1/_4$ cup (60 ml) ice water

Filling
2 teaspoons oil
1 medium-sized red onion, cut into thin strips
1 teaspoon balsamic vinegar
$1^1/_2$ lbs (750 g) ramps or scallions (spring onions)
11 to 12 egg yolks (about 1 cup)
$1^1/_2$ cups (375 ml) heavy (double) cream
Pinch of ground nutmeg
4 oz (125 g) grated mild cheese, such as Monterey Jack, *queso fresco*, farmer or goat cheese
Salt and freshly ground black pepper to taste

1 To make the Tart Shell, combine the flour and salt in the bowl of an electric mixer. Add the butter and using the whisk attachment, combine the mixture on a slow speed. When small chunks the size of rice form, add the yolks and increase the speed. Strain in ice water and mix until combined. Allow dough to rest in plastic wrap overnight or freeze it for later use. Bring dough to room temperature before using.
2 Preheat the oven to 350°F (180°C, gas mark 4).
3 Roll out the dough on a lightly floured surface to a thickness of $^1/_8$ in ($^1/_3$ cm) and place it in an 8-in (20-cm) tart or pie pan. Cover the pie dough with foil and fill the pan with dried beans or rice to keep the dough from bubbling. Bake for 12 minutes, or until the crust is golden brown and the center is cooked. Carefully take off the foil and weights. Let the crust cool at room temperature.
4 To make the Filling, heat the oil in a sauté pan, add the onion and vinegar, and sauté over medium heat until the onions are browned. Remove the onion and set aside. Add the ramps to the pan with a little more oil and salt to keep them green. Cook until they're tender then set aside to cool.
5 Raise the oven temperature to 375°F (190°C, gas mark 5).
6 In a mixing bowl, combine the ramps and onion. In another bowl, whisk the egg yolks, cream and nutmeg.
7 To assemble, sprinkle the cheese on the bottom of the tart shell and add the onion mixture. Pour in the egg mixture, making sure not to fill the shell completely. Season with the salt and pepper. Cover the tart with foil and bake in the oven until the eggs are firm, 35 to 40 minutes. Remove the foil during the last 2 minutes so that the tart will lightly brown. Cool tart slightly before serving.

Serves 6 to 8   Preparation time: 45 mins + overnight for dough to rest
Cooking time: 1 hour

Spanish Rice   Rice with Green Chile, Olives and Tomatoes

1 cup (200 g) uncooked long-grain
  white rice
1 tablespoon oil
1 medium-sized onion, chopped
1 clove garlic, minced
1¹/₂ cups (375 ml) chicken broth
¹/₂ cup (100 g) roasted, peeled,
  deseeded and chopped New
  Mexican green chiles (about 5)
4 canned tomatoes, chopped,
  or 1 medium fresh tomato,
  peeled and chopped
4 tablespoons tomato purée
4 tablespoons sliced black olives
2 teaspoons dried oregano
¹/₄ teaspoon ground cumin
Salt to taste
Chopped jalapeño chiles, to garnish

1 Wash the rice in a couple of changes of water until the water runs clear, then drain. Set aside.

2 In a heavy skillet, heat the oil over medium-high heat, add the rice, and sauté until it turns opaque and starts to brown, about 3 minutes. Stir in the onion and garlic, and cook for a few more minutes.

3 In a saucepan over high heat, bring the broth to a boil. Add the remaining ingredients and the sautéed rice, bring back to a boil, and stir a couple of times. Reduce the heat, cover, and simmer for 20 to 30 minutes, or until the rice is tender. Remove from the heat.

4 Fluff the rice with a fork, garnish with the chiles and serve hot.

Serves 4   Preparation time: 30 mins   Cooking time: 40 mins

Green Rice   Arroz Verde

This dish gets its name and color from the green of tomatillo, jalapeño and cilantro.

1 cup (200 g) uncooked long-grain
  white rice
3 jalapeño chiles, diced
1 can (1 lb/500 g) tomatillos, drained
1 clove garlic
¹/₄ teaspoon ground cumin
1¹/₂ cups (375 ml) chicken broth
2 tablespoons oil
¹/₂ cup (75 g) minced onion
1 tablespoon chopped fresh cilantro
  (coriander leaves)
Sliced jalapeño chiles, to garnish

1 Wash the rice in a couple of changes of water until the water runs clear, then drain. Set aside.

2 Place the chiles, tomatillos, garlic and cumin in a blender or food processor, add 1 cup (250 ml) of the broth, and purée the mixture until it's smooth. Add additional broth to make 2 cups (500 ml) of ground ingredients.

3 In a heavy skillet, heat the oil over medium-high heat, add the onion, and sauté until it's soft, 2 to 3 minutes. Add the rice and sauté for a couple of minutes, or until the rice starts to turn opaque. Remove from the heat.

4 Bring the broth mixture to a boil in a saucepan and add sautéed rice. Reduce the heat, cover, and simmer until all the liquid is absorbed, 20 to 30 minutes. Remove the pan from the heat.

5 Lightly toss the rice with the chopped cilantro, garnish with sliced jalapeños, and serve hot.

Serves 4   Preparation time: 20 mins   Cooking time: 40 mins

Jalapeño Cheddar Cornbread

Heating the chiles in the milk takes away some of their bite, but if the bread is too spicy for you, decrease the amount of chile or substitute a milder New Mexican green chile. For an even milder bread, green or red bell peppers may be used.

3 tablespoons minced jalapeño chiles (2 to 3 chiles)
1 large onion, minced
1½ cups (375 ml) buttermilk
1 cup (200 g) yellow cornmeal
1 cup (150 g) flour
2 teaspoons sugar
1 teaspoon baking soda
1 teaspoon baking powder
1 teaspoon salt
¼ teaspoon garlic powder
2 eggs, beaten
1 cup (125 g) grated Cheddar cheese

1 Preheat the oven to 400°F (200°C, gas mark 6) and lightly oil a 9 x 9-in (22 x 22-cm) pan.
2 In a small saucepan over low heat, cook the jalapeños and onion in the buttermilk for 3 to 5 minutes. Remove the pan from the heat and allow the mixture to cool.
3 In a large mixing bowl, combine all the dry ingredients. Mix the eggs and cheese together in another bowl. Stir in the buttermilk mixture. Pour the liquid ingredients into the dry ones and quickly mix them. Pour the batter into the oiled pan. Bake for 40 minutes, or until it turns golden brown, and a toothpick inserted in the center comes out clean.
4 Cool the cornbread slightly, slice it and serve hot or at room temperature, accompanied by a flavored butter.

Makes nine 3-in (8-cm) pieces   Preparation time: 10 mins   Cooking time: 45 mins

Chile-flavored Butters

These compound butters can be used in a variety of ways. They keep indefinitely in the freezer, so keep several on hand.

Orange Zest Red Chile Butter
2 tablespoons grated orange zest
2 teaspoons orange juice
2 teaspoons ground red chile, such as New Mexican, piquín or chile de Árbol
1 lb (500 g) unsalted butter (4 sticks), softened

Roasted Green Chile and Spring Onion Butter
3 New Mexican green chiles, roasted, peeled, deseeded and minced
4 scallions (spring onions), finely sliced, some of the greens included
¼ teaspoon garlic powder
1 lb (500 g) unsalted butter (4 sticks), softened

Combine all the ingredients in a bowl and mix them thoroughly. Allow the butter to sit at room temperature for 1 hour to blend the flavors. Chill the butter before serving.

Makes 1 lb (500 g) each   Preparation time: 1 hour 15 mins

Corn Tortillas

2 cups (350 g) masa harina
$^1/_2$ teaspoon salt
$1^1/_3$ cups (350 ml) very warm water

1 Combine the masa harina and salt in a large bowl and add 1 cup (250 ml) of the warm water. Work the water in with your hands, lightly kneading the dough with the heel of your hand for 3 to 5 minutes until the mixture is smooth. Add more water if necessary. The dough should be very soft, not sticky or elastic like bread dough.
2 Divide the dough into 15 portions and roll them into balls, $1^1/_2$ in (4 cm) in diameter. Cover with plastic wrap and let them rest for 20 to 30 minutes.
3 Place a sheet of plastic wrap on the bottom of a tortilla press. Place a ball of masa on the press, a little off-center towards the hinge. Cover the dough with another sheet of plastic wrap and press down to form the tortilla.
4 Heat a dry comal, heavy skillet, or griddle until it is medium-hot. Carefully slip the tortilla onto the comal. The tortilla should just sizzle as it touches the pan and shouldn't take longer than 2 minutes to cook. Turn the tortilla over and cook it slightly longer on the other side, or until it browns lightly in spots and the top begins to puff. Remove the tortilla and keep it warm in a towel for 10 to 15 minutes to let it finish cooking and become soft and pliable.

Note: It's important that the masa be the right consistency. If the dough is too dry, the tortillas will be rather thick and have a grainy, crumbly edge. They also won't puff up much and will be heavy. If the dough is too wet you won't be able to form a tortilla or remove it from the plastic wrap. Both problems are easy to remedy. Just add a little more water or masa harina, whichever is needed.

Makes 15   Preparation time: 30 mins + 30 mins for dough to rest
Cooking time: 20 mins

Clockwise from top: Pueblo Bread (page 97), Fried Bread (page 97), white and blue Corn Tortillas and Flour Tortillas (page 96). These breads are served in an antique Maidu Indian winnowing tray.

Flour Tortillas

2 cups (300 g) flour
1/2 teaspoon salt
1 teaspoon baking powder (optional)
3 to 4 tablespoons lard or vegetable
  shortening, or a mixture of the two
3/4 cup (175 ml) very warm water

1 Sift the dry ingredients into a large bowl. Work in the shortening with your fingertips until it is evenly mixed. Pour 2/3 of the water over the mixture and mix it in with a fork. The dough will have large lumps. Add the remaining water, if needed, and gather the dough into a ball.

2 Knead the dough well for 5 minutes. The dough should be medium stiff, not as soft as bread dough but also not firm. Divide the dough into 12 portions and roll them into balls. Cover with a towel and let them rest for 20 minutes.

3 Lightly flour a surface, flatten out one of the dough balls and roll it until it is thin. Heat a dry comal, heavy skillet or griddle to medium hot. Lay the tortilla onto the griddle—you should hear a faint sizzle when it first hits the cooking surface. Cook until bubbles form on the top and brown spots appear underneath, 30 to 45 seconds. Turn over the tortilla and cook it for an additional 30 to 45 seconds. Be sure not to overcook it, or the tortilla will become crisp. Remove the tortilla and cover it with a towel to keep it warm.

Makes 12   Preparation time: 30 mins + 20 mins for dough to rest
Cooking time: 15 mins

Anasazi Flatbread   Flynt Payne, Inn of the Anasazi

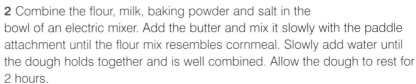

8 oz (250 g) shiitake mushrooms,
  thinly sliced
4 tablespoons minced red onion
1/2 teaspoon thinly sliced fresh sage
3/4 cup (175 ml) olive oil
2 1/2 cups (375 g) flour
2 tablespoons powdered dry milk
2 teaspoons baking powder
1/2 teaspoon kosher salt, plus
  additional salt for seasoning
3 tablespoons butter
Water

1 Over medium heat, sauté the mushrooms, onion and sage in 2 teaspoons of the oil until they are soft. Remove from the heat and allow them to cool.

2 Combine the flour, milk, baking powder and salt in the bowl of an electric mixer. Add the butter and mix it slowly with the paddle attachment until the flour mix resembles cornmeal. Slowly add water until the dough holds together and is well combined. Allow the dough to rest for 2 hours.

3 On a lightly floured surface, roll out the dough to a thickness of 1/4 in (1/2 cm). Cut out 5-in (13-cm) circles.

4 Heat the remaining oil in a skillet until it's hot, and fry the circles until they're browned. Carefully remove them, drain and season with kosher salt if desired.

Makes 12   Preparation time: 20 mins + 2 hours for dough to rest
Cooking time: 15 mins

Pueblo Bread

This hearty bread is baked in the adobe beehive-shaped ovens called "hornos." Before baking, a fire is made inside the oven and is allowed to burn itself out. The ashes are swept out, the bread is placed in the oven, and the opening is sealed to allow the bread to bake. To achieve a nice crisp crust in a conventional oven, gently mist the bread with water from a spray bottle a couple of times as it bakes.

2 tablespoons active dry yeast
2 cups (500 ml) warm water
$1/2$ teaspoon sugar
2 tablespoons melted butter, cooled
1 teaspoon salt
$4^1/2$ cups (540 g) unbleached bread
   flour

1 In a large bowl, dissolve the yeast in $1/2$ cup (125 ml) of the warm water (110°F/45°C) and stir in the sugar. Let it sit for 10 minutes.
2 Stir the butter and salt into the yeast mixture. Add 1 cup (120 g) of the bread flour and beat well. Add some of the remaining $1^1/2$ cups (375 ml) of the warm water, then some flour, beating the mixture well after each addition. Add the remaining flour and water, alternating between wet and dry.
3 Turn the dough onto a lightly floured surface and knead it for 10 minutes, or until the dough is smooth and elastic. Gather the dough into a ball and place it in an oiled bowl. Cover the bowl with a towel and let the dough rise in a warm place until it has doubled, about 1 hour.
4 Punch the dough down and knead it for 5 minutes. Divide the dough in half and place in 2 smaller oiled ovenproof bowls, turning once so the tops are oiled. Cover them with a towel and let them rise for 30 minutes.
5 Preheat the oven to 400°F (200°C, gas mark 6). Bake the dough for 45 to 50 minutes, or until the loaves are lightly browned and sound hollow when tapped.

Makes 2 loaves   Preparation time: 30 mins + 1 hour 30 mins for dough to rise
Cooking time: 50 mins

Fried Bread   Sopaipillas

Sopaipillas, or "little pillows," are squares or triangles of bread that puff up when fried. After tortillas, they are the most commonly served bread in New Mexico. They are served with traditional meals, accompanied by a dispenser of honey. The combination of the sugar in the honey and the starch of the bread cuts the heat of hot chiles. To eat sopaipillas, tear or bite off a corner of the bread, pour in the honey and enjoy.

2 cups (300 ml) flour
2 teaspoons baking powder
$1/2$ teaspoon salt
2 tablespoons butter
$2/3$ cup (150 ml) warm water
Oil for deep-frying

1 In a large bowl, combine the flour, baking powder and salt. Cut in the butter until the flour resembles coarse meal. Add the water, a little at a time, until the dough is moist and can be gathered into a ball. Knead it a couple of times, cover it with a towel, and let it sit for 30 minutes.
2 On a lightly floured board, roll out the dough until it forms a rectangle $1/4$ in ($1/2$ cm) thick. Cut into 2 x 3-in (5 x 8-cm) rectangles.
3 In a deep pot or fryer, heat the oil to 400°F (200°C). Place the sopaipillas, 3 or 4 at a time, in the hot oil and spoon a little oil over the top of each to start them puffing. When they have browned on one side, 20 to 30 seconds, turn them over and brown the other side. Turn them only once. Remove and drain them on paper towels. Serve immediately.

Note: For very light sopaipillas, do not handle the dough more than necessary.

Makes 20   Preparation time: 20 mins + 30 mins for dough to rest
Cooking time: 15 mins

Taco-nolis   Katharine Kagel, Cafe Pasqual's

These are a Santa Fe takeoff of cannoli, the renowned Italian dessert.
This dessert is shaped like a taco. The tequila-flavored ricotta is topped
with pistachio nuts to imitate the avocado, dried cherries for tomatoes,
chocolate chips for the ground beef, and colored coconut to represent
lettuce and cheese. Delicious and hilarious!

Shells
1 tablespoon sugar
$1^1/_2$ tablespoons butter
2 cups (300 g) flour
1 egg yolk
$^1/_4$ cup (60 ml) white wine
3 cups (750 ml) canola oil

Filling
2 cups (250 g) Ricotta cheese, drained
$^3/_4$ cup (150 g) powdered sugar
$1^1/_2$ cups (375 ml) heavy (thick) whipping cream
$^1/_2$ teaspoon vanilla
$1^1/_2$ tablespoons tequila

Toppings
10 to 12 fresh cherries, or 2 tablespoons dried cherries
1 package shredded coconut
Orange and green food coloring
$^1/_3$ cup (50 g) pistachios
1 package tiny chocolate chips

1 Prepare the Shells by blending the sugar and butter with the flour and
adding the egg yolk and white wine. Divide the dough into 10 pieces and
roll each into a ball. Using a pasta machine, roll out the dough balls into
thin circles about 5 to 6 in (13 to 15 cm) in diameter.
2 In a stockpot or fryer, heat the oil to 370°F (190°C), or until a pinch of
dough dropped into the oil bobs to the surface immediately. Drape each
dough circle over a taco, or use tongs to fold it in half, keeping it open
enough for the Filling, and fry until golden brown. Drain the taco-nolis and
set aside on paper towels.
3 To make the Filling, whisk together the Ricotta and sugar. Using an electric
mixer, whip the cream until it's stiff. Fold the vanilla and tequila carefully into
the whipped cream, then fold in the Ricotta mixture. Refrigerate the mixture
until you're ready to fill the taco-nolis.
4 To make the Toppings, pit and discard the stems of the cherries and cut them
into quarters. Mix $^1/_2$ cup (50 g) of the coconut with 2 or 3 drops of orange
food coloring to make the "cheese," and mix another $^1/_2$ cup of coconut
with 2 or 3 drops of green food coloring for the "lettuce"; toss to color the
coconut. Rub the skin off the pistachios to make the "avocado."
5 Spoon the Filling into the tacos and sprinkle on the Toppings. Serve
immediately.

Makes 10   Preparation time: 1 hour   Cooking time: 30 mins

Arroz Con Leche   Maurice Zeck, La Fonda

4 tablespoons raisins
2 tablespoons brandy
$^3/_4$ cup (150 g) uncooked white rice,
  rinsed and drained (page 31)
$2^1/_2$ cups (625 ml) milk
1 cinnamon stick, 3 in (8 cm) long
Zest of 1 lemon, peeled in wide strips
2 tablespoons vanilla
3 tablespoons brown sugar
2 egg yolks
2 tablespoons sugar

Toasted Banana Sauce
1 banana
2 cups (500 ml) half-and-half (pouring
  cream)
2 tablespoons sugar
1 egg yolk
1 tablespoon banana liqueur

Spiced Peaches
4 fresh peaches, sliced
1 teaspoon ground cinnamon
1 tablespoon brown sugar
Pinch of ground nutmeg
2 tablespoons peach schnapps

1 To make the Toasted Banana Sauce, preheat the oven to 400°F (200°C, gas mark 6). Place the banana on a baking sheet and toast in the oven until browned. Purée the toasted banana in a blender until smooth.
2 Combine the half-and-half and $1^1/_2$ tablespoons of the sugar in a saucepan. Heat over medium heat until just below boiling. Remove from the heat. In a small bowl, whisk the egg yolk with the remaining sugar. Add 2 tablespoons of the hot half-and-half to temper the yolks, then stir the yolk mixture into the rest of the half-and-half. Return the saucepan to the heat and cook until the mixture coats the back of a spoon. Stir in the liqueur and remove from the heat. Add the banana purée to the sauce and mix well. Refrigerate for 1 hour.
3 Prepare the Spiced Peaches by combining all the ingredients and tossing well. Set aside.
4 To make the pudding, place the raisins in a bowl and cover them with the brandy to plump them up. Combine the rice, milk, cinnamon, lemon zest, vanilla and brown sugar in a medium saucepan. Simmer over low heat, covered, until the rice is cooked, 12 to 15 minutes. When the rice is done, remove the cinnamon stick and lemon zest. Add the brandy and raisins to the mixture.
5 Whisk together the egg yolks and the rest of the sugar and stir the mixture into the cooked rice. Continue to cook the rice mixture, stirring often for 5 to 10 minutes, until thickened. Be careful not to overcook.
6 Place the rice pudding in a glass serving bowl, drizzle the Toasted Banana Sauce over the top, and garnish with the Spiced Peaches.

Serves 4   Preparation time: 20 mins + 1 hour refrigeration   Cooking time: 45 mins

Capriotada with Raspberry Sauce and Whipped Cream

Maurice Zeck, La Fonda

2 tablespoons butter or lard
3 to 4 slices white bread
3 oz (85 g) semisweet chocolate, melted
$^1/_4$ cup (50 g) sugar
1 teaspoon ground cinnamon
$^1/_3$ cup (50 g) grated Asadero cheese
1 tablespoon chopped walnuts
1 tablespoon chopped peanuts
2 teaspoons pine nuts
1 tablespoon raisins

Raspberry Sauce
4 cups (720 g) fresh raspberries
$^1/_4$ cup (60 ml) orange juice
2 tablespoons butter
2 tablespoons sugar
1 tablespoon orange liqueur
1 tablespoon raspberry liqueur
2 tablespoons cornstarch mixed with
  3 tablespoons water (optional)

Nutmeg Cream
1 cup (250 ml) heavy (double) cream
2 to 3 tablespoons sugar
$^1/_2$ teaspoon grated nutmeg

1 Preheat the oven to 250°F (120°C, gas mark $^1/_4$).
2 In a heavy skillet, heat the butter until it's hot, add the bread, and fry until it's golden. Remove the bread and drain it on paper towels.
3 In a heavy saucepan over medium-high heat, add the chocolate, sugar, cinnamon and 1 cup (250 ml) water. Bring it to a boil, reduce the heat, and simmer while stirring to form a syrup, about 5 minutes.
4 Lightly oil a 9 x 12-in (25 x 30-cm) baking dish or pan. Layer the bread, cheese, syrup, nuts and raisins in the pan; cover the pan and bake for 30 to 45 minutes, or until golden. Remove the pan and let it cool.
5 To make the Raspberry Sauce, combine all the ingredients except the cornstarch and water in a saucepan and bring to a boil. Reduce the heat and simmer for 15 minutes. Remove and strain. If the sauce is too thin, return it to the pan, heat and stir in the cornstarch mixture and thicken it to the desired consistency.
6 To make the Nutmeg Cream, whip the cream with the sugar and nutmeg until it's thick.
7 To assemble, place the pudding on a plate or in a bowl. Drizzle the Raspberry Sauce over the pudding, top with the Nutmeg Cream and serve at room temperature.

Serves 4   Preparation time: 30 mins   Cooking time: 1 hour 15 mins

Cajeta Sundae with Toasted Piñon Cookie   Andrew MacLauchlan, Coyote Cafe

1 tub (1 liter) vanilla ice cream

Cajeta Caramel
4 cups (1 liter) evaporated goat's milk
$1^1/_2$ cups (375 ml) milk
4 teaspoons cornstarch
$^1/_2$ teaspoon baking soda
$1^1/_2$ cups (300 g) sugar

Piñon Cookie
$^1/_4$ cup (60 g) butter
$^1/_4$ cup (40 g) brown sugar
$^1/_4$ cup (50 g) sugar
$^3/_4$ cup (120 g) piñon nuts, lightly
  roasted and ground
1 egg
$^1/_2$ teaspoon vanilla
$^1/_2$ teaspoon baking soda
$^1/_3$ cup (50 g) flour

Serves 6
Preparation time: 30 mins
Cooking time: 1 hour 45 mins

1 Prepare the Cajeta Caramel by combining both milks in a large saucepan and bring to a boil over medium-high heat. Reduce the heat and simmer.
2 Place the cornstarch and baking soda in a small bowl. Whisk in some of the hot milk, stirring until the cornstarch mixture dissolves. Whisk this mixture back into the milk in the saucepan and continue to simmer over low heat.
3 In another saucepan, heat the sugar over high heat, stirring continuously as it melts and turns brown (caramelizes), 8 to 10 minutes. Reduce the heat to medium and continue to stir until the sugar is evenly melted, a deep amber color, and smoking lightly. Ladle the hot milk into the caramel; be very careful because the mixture will bubble up violently. Stir the milk in until the mixture no longer bubbles up when the hot milk is added. Return this caramel-and-milk mixture to the other saucepan and simmer to reduce it by about half, approximately 1 hour. Cool the mixture over ice.
4 Preheat the oven to 350°F (180°C, gas mark 4).
5 To make the Piñon Cookie, cream the butter and both sugars together in a mixing bowl. Add all other other ingredients and mix thoroughly. Spread the batter into desired shapes, about $^1/_{16}$ in (1 mm) thick, on a nonstick baking pan with a spatula. Bake the cookies for 12 to 14 minutes, remove from the oven, and let them cool.
6 To serve, place a Piñon Cookie on each plate and stack 2 scoops of the ice cream on top, then drizzle with the Cajeta Caramel. Stick another Piñon Cookie in the ice cream and serve.

Granita   Kelly Rogers, La Casa Sena

Granitas are intentionally made to have a grainy texture similar to shaved ice. This frozen fruit ice is a popular choice at La Casa Sena and may be served as an intermezzo (something eaten between courses to cleanse the palate), a dessert or even a cocktail! It's so easy to make. This recipe is for three different granitas; use a different juice for each one.

2 cups (500 ml) freshly squeezed watermelon juice, grapefruit juice or prickly pear cactus juice
1 jalapeño chile, deseeded and finely chopped
Juice of half a lime
4 sprigs of mint, to garnish

Simple Syrup
$^1/_3$ cup (65 g) sugar
$^2/_3$ cup (150 ml) water

1 Make the Simple Syrup by combining the sugar and water in a small saucepan. Simmer over low heat until the sugar has dissolved and the mixture is clear. Raise the heat and boil for 1 minute.
2 Combine the fruit juice, jalapeño, Simple Syrup and lime juice in a saucepan and simmer for 5 minutes over medium heat to incorporate the Simple Syrup. Do not boil or reduce the sauce.
3 Pour the mixture into a shallow metal dish and place it in the freezer. Every hour, stir the mixture to cause ice crystals to form. After a few hours, the granita will form into a granular substance similar to shaved ice.
4 Serve the granita in chilled martini glasses with a sprig of mint. If you desire, splash a little tequila, vodka or champagne over it and serve it as a cocktail.

Note: To juice a watermelon, place the "flesh" of the melon in a medium-mesh strainer and force it through with a ladle or wooden spoon into a bowl.

Serves 4   Preparation time: 20 mins + 3 hours to freeze   Cooking time: 10 mins

Vanilla Flan   Santa Fe School of Cooking

1¼ cups (250 g) sugar
1 cup (250 ml) milk
2 cups (500 ml) heavy (double)
  cream
2 large eggs
3 large egg yolks
2 teaspoons pure vanilla extract

1 Preheat the oven to 325°F (160°C, gas mark 3).
2 Melt 1 cup (200 g) of the sugar in a small, dry skillet over medium-high heat. As the sugar caramelizes, press the unmelted sugar into the liquefied part with the bottom of a heavy spoon. Reduce the heat to medium and continue cooking until you have a clear, deep amber liquid, 8 to 10 minutes. Remove from the heat and immediately pour equal amounts of the caramel syrup into six ½-cup (125-ml) ramekins, tilting the cups to distribute the syrup evenly on the bottoms and sides.
3 In a saucepan over medium heat, combine the milk, cream and the remaining ¼ cup (50 g) of sugar. Heat the mixture over medium-high heat until it's hot but not boiling, stirring to dissolve the sugar. Remove the pan from the heat and let the mixture cool slightly.
4 In a small bowl, whisk the eggs and yolks until they're well blended. Slowly pour the eggs into the heated milk mixture, whisking constantly. Stir in the vanilla. Place the ramekins with the caramel syrup in a baking pan and divide the milk mixture evenly among the ramekins. Fill the pan with boiling water to about three-quarters up the sides of the ramekins. In the oven, bake the custard in the water bath for 35 to 45 minutes, or until it no longer trembles when moved. Remove the ramekins from the oven and set aside to cool, then chill covered in the refrigerator for 3 to 4 hours.
5 To serve, unmold the custard by running a knife around the edge of the ramekins and transfer the custard onto dessert plates.

Serves 6   Preparation time: 20 mins + 4 hours to chill
Cooking time: 1 hour 15 mins

Natillas   Santa Fe School of Cooking

This dish is similar to the classic French dessert "floating islands"—a rich custard with spoonfuls of meringue on top—though with some differences. In Santa Fe, the meringue is folded into the custard, which is then stabilized with flour. This technique was originally used to extend eggs, an item that was in short supply for the early Santa Fe settlers.

2 eggs, separated
2 tablespoons flour
2 cups (500 ml) heavy (double)
  cream, divided
¼ cup (50 g) plus 2 tablespoons
  sugar, divided
Pinch of salt
¾ teaspoon vanilla, preferably
  Mexican vanilla
Freshly grated nutmeg or cinnamon

1 In a bowl, make a paste of the egg yolks, flour and ½ cup (125 ml) of the cream.
2 In a saucepan, combine ¼ cup (50 g) of the sugar and the salt with the remaining cream and bring the mixture to just below boiling. Whisk the scalded cream gradually into the egg mixture and place it in a double boiler over simmering water. Cook the mixture slowly, stirring constantly, until it thickens, about 20 minutes. Remove the mixture from the heat, mix in the vanilla and allow the mixture to cool. The recipe may be made ahead of time to this point.
3 Beat the egg whites with the remaining 2 tablespoons of the sugar until they're stiff and shiny but not dry. Fold the egg whites into the cooled custard. Transfer to a serving bowl and sprinkle with freshly grated nutmeg or cinnamon. Serve immediately.

Serves 4 to 6   Preparation time: 30 mins + 20 mins to cool   Cooking time: 25 mins

Empanaditas with Apricot Pecan Filling
Dessert Turnovers

Empanaditas are little filled pies, or turnovers, that are found in one form or another all around the world. These may be baked with or without a sugar topping, or deep-fried and dusted with powdered sugar before serving. The filling may be puréed or left with some texture. If you do purée it, do so before adding nuts and eliminate the raisins.

Filling
1 lb (500 g) dried apricots, quartered
1 cup (200 g) sugar, or more to taste
$1/2$ teaspoon salt
$1/4$ teaspoon ground nutmeg
4 tablespoons raisins
4 tablespoons chopped pecans

Dough
2 cups (300 g) flour
1 teaspoon salt
$2/3$ cup (150 ml) vegetable shortening
4 to 5 tablespoons cold water
1 egg, separated

1 Prepare the Filling by placing the apricots in a saucepan over medium heat and covering them with water. Add the sugar and simmer until the apricots are very soft and start to break down, 20 to 25 minutes. Add more water if necessary. Stir in the remaining ingredients, remove the pan from the heat, and allow the Filling to cool.
2 Preheat the oven to 400°F (200°C, gas mark 6).
3 To make the Dough, combine the flour and salt in a large mixing bowl. Cut the shortening into the dry ingredients using a pastry cutter or two forks. The mixture should resemble coarse cornmeal. Add the cold water, one tablespoon at a time, and lightly toss with a fork to incorporate it. Add only enough water for the Dough to hold together and be gathered into a ball.
4 Lightly beat the egg white, then beat the egg yolk separately with 1 tablespoon of water.
5 Gently roll out the Dough on a lightly floured surface to $1/4$ in ($1/2$ cm) thick. Using a round cookie cutter or juice glass, cut out circles about $2^1/2$ in (6 cm) in diameter. Place a spoonful of the Filling off-center on each circle. Brush the edges of each circle with the egg white, fold it in half, and crimp the edges to seal.
6 Brush the empanaditas with the egg yolk, place them on a lightly oiled baking pan, and bake for 10 to 12 minutes, or until golden. Cool the empanaditas on a rack before serving.

Note: If you're short of time, ready-made pie crusts may be used for the pastry, but don't roll it out before cutting it.

Makes 24   Preparation time: 1 hour   Cooking time: 40 mins

Maria's Margarita
Al Lucero, Maria's New Mexican Kitchen

The origin of the margarita is uncertain, but many stories are told. One is that a bartender in Palm Springs invented it just after World War II and named it after his girlfriend. Another is that in the late forties a woman named Margarita Sames concocted it while throwing a party at her hacienda in Acapulco. Yet another claims that the owner of a Los Angeles bar and restaurant called the Tail o'the Cock was the originator. No matter who created the drink, it is responsible for the United States becoming the largest consumer of tequila. It imports more than double what is drunk in Mexico! Maria's New Mexican Kitchen is well known for serving the most authentic and best margaritas—at least according to Robert Redford. Maria's Special Margarita is touted as the best-selling hand-shaken margarita in Santa Fe.

1 lemon or lime wedge
Saucer of kosher salt, about $^1/_4$ in ($^1/_2$ cm) deep
$1^1/_4$ fl oz (40 ml) Jose Cuervo Silver tequila
$^3/_4$ fl oz (25 ml) Bols triple sec
$1^1/_2$ fl oz (45 ml) freshly squeezed lemon or lime juice

1 Rub the lemon or lime around the rim of a margarita glass. Dip the rim of the glass into the salt and rotate it until the salt has collected on the glass.
2 Pour the tequila, triple sec and lemon or lime juice into a 16-fl oz (500-ml) cocktail shaker glass full of ice. Place the shaker over the glass and shake it for about 5 seconds. Pour the drink into the salted glass and serve immediately.

Makes 1   Preparation time: 5 mins

The Elizabeth II

This drink was created one night after a waitress described the ingredients of a margarita to a customer. He was a fan of orange liqueurs and asked if they could be substituted or included. They were, and a new margarita was born. The name Elizabeth II refers to the waitress and the two orange liqueurs.

1 lemon or lime wedge
Saucer of kosher salt, about $^1/_4$ in ($^1/_2$ cm) deep
$1^1/_4$ fl oz (40 ml) El Tesoro Plata tequila
$^1/_2$ fl oz (15 ml) Grand Marnier
$^1/_2$ fl oz (15 ml) Cointreau
$1^1/_2$ fl oz (45 ml) freshly squeezed lemon or lime juice

1 Rub the lemon or lime around the rim of a margarita glass. Dip the rim of the glass into the salt and rotate it until the salt has collected on the glass.
2 Pour the tequila, Grand Marnier, Cointreau and lemon or lime juice into a 16-fl oz (500-ml) cocktail shaker glass full of ice. Place a stainless-steel cocktail shaker over the glass and shake it vigorously for about 5 seconds. Pour the drink into the salted glass and serve immediately.

Makes 1   Preparation time: 5 mins

Maria's Famous La Ultima Margarita

Up until the time this margarita was created, most tequila connoisseurs would only drink super-premium tequila straight. To get the full flavor of this drink, there should be no substitutions.

1 lemon or lime wedge
Saucer of kosher salt, about $^1/_4$ in ($^1/_2$ cm) deep
$1^1/_4$ fl oz (40 ml) El Tesoro 100 Percent Blue Agave Plata tequila
$^3/_4$ fl oz (25 ml) Cointreau
$1^1/_2$ fl oz (45 ml) freshly squeezed lemon or lime juice

Makes 1
Preparation time: 5 mins

1 Rub the lemon or lime wedge around the rim of a margarita glass. Dip the rim of the glass into the saucer of salt and rotate it until the salt has collected on the glass.
2 Pour the tequila, Cointreau and lemon or lime juice into a 16-fl oz (500-ml) cocktail shaker glass full of ice. Place a stainless-steel cocktail shaker over the glass and shake it vigorously for about 5 seconds. Pour the drink into the salted glass and serve immediately.

El Amor de Oro Margarita

This drink, named "The Golden Love," is one of the most elegant margaritas served at Maria's.

1 lemon or lime wedge
Saucer of kosher salt, about $^1/_4$ in ($^1/_2$ cm) deep
$1^1/_4$ fl oz (40 ml) Centinela 100 Percent Blue Agave Tres Años tequila
$^3/_4$ fl oz (25 ml) Cointreau
$1^1/_2$ fl oz (45 ml) freshly squeezed lemon or lime juice

Makes 1
Preparation time: 5 mins

1 Rub the lemon or lime wedge around the rim of a margarita glass. Dip the rim of the glass into the saucer of salt and rotate it until the salt has collected on the glass.
2 Pour the tequila, Cointreau and lemon or lime juice into a 16-fl oz (500-ml) cocktail shaker glass full of ice. Place a stainless-steel cocktail shaker over the glass and shake it vigorously for about 5 seconds. Pour the drink into the salted glass and serve immediately.

Chimayó Cocktail

Chimayó is a small village just north of Santa Fe that was settled by the Spanish in the seventeenth century. It's famous for its chile, apples and the healing properties of the holy dirt that is found in the *santuario* (church) in the village. Every Easter, thousands of people from all over the state make a pilgrimage and walk to the shrine in Chimayó. The Jaramillo family, which owns the picturesque Rancho de Chimayó restaurant, invented this cocktail to promote both the village and its apples.

$1^1/_4$ fl oz (40 ml) tequila
$^1/_4$ fl oz ($1^1/_2$ teaspoons) crème de cassis
1 fl oz (30 ml) fresh apple cider or apple juice
$^1/_4$ fl oz ($1^1/_2$ teaspoons) freshly squeezed lemon juice
1 red apple wedge

Makes 1
Preparation time: 5 mins

1 Fill a double old-fashioned glass with ice.
2 Pour the tequila, crème de cassis, apple cider and lemon juice over the ice and stir.
3 Garnish the glass with an apple wedge and serve.

24-Karat Gold Reserve

Three hundred and fifty years in the making! This combination of 200th Anniversary Hand Crafted Jose Cuervo Añejo 100% Agave Barrel Select tequila and 150th Anniversary Cuveé Speciale Grand Marnier are the basis of the "most elegant Margarita in the world."

1 lemon or lime wedge
Saucer of kosher salt, about $^1/_4$ in ($^1/_2$ cm) deep
$1^1/_4$ fl oz (40 ml) 200th Anniversary Hand Crafted Jose Cuervo Añejo 100% Agave Barrel Select tequila
$^3/_4$ fl oz (25 ml) 150th Anniversary Cuveé Speciale Grand Marnier
$1^1/_2$ fl oz (45 ml) freshly squeezed lemon or lime juice

Makes 1
Preparation time: 5 mins

1 Rub the lemon or lime wedge around the rim of a margarita glass. Dip the rim of the glass into the saucer of salt and rotate it until the salt has collected on the glass.
2 Pour the tequila, Grand Marnier and juice into a 16-fl oz (500-ml) cocktail shaker glass full of ice. Place a stainless-steel cocktail shaker over the glass and shake it vigorously for about 5 seconds. Pour the drink into the salted glass and serve immediately.

Complete list of recipes

Measurements and conversions

Measurements in this book are given in volume as far as possible. Teaspoon, tablespoon and cup measurements should be level, not heaped, unless otherwise indicated. Australian readers please note that the standard Australian measuring spoon is larger than the UK or American spoon by 5 ml, so use $3/4$ tablespoon instead of a full tablespoon when following the recipes.

Liquid Conversions

Imperial	Metric	US cups
$1/2$ fl oz	15 ml	1 tablespoon
1 fl oz	30 ml	$1/8$ cup
2 fl oz	60 ml	$1/4$ cup
3 fl oz	85 ml	$1/3$ cup
4 fl oz	125 ml	$1/2$ cup
5 fl oz	150 ml	$2/3$ cup
6 fl oz	175 ml	$3/4$ cup
8 fl oz	250 ml	1 cup
12 fl oz	375 ml	$1 1/2$ cups
16 fl oz	500 ml	2 cups
1 quart	1 liter	4 cups

Note: 1 UK pint = 20 fl oz
1 US pint = 16 fl oz

Solid Weight Conversions

Imperial	Metric
$1/2$ oz	15 g
1 oz	28 g
$1 1/2$ oz	45 g
2 oz	60 g
3 oz	85 g
$3 1/2$ oz	100 g
4 oz ($1/4$ lb)	125 g
5 oz	150 g
6 oz	175 g
7 oz	200 g
8 oz ($1/2$ lb)	225 g
9 oz	260 g
10 oz	300 g
16 oz (1 lb)	450 g
32 oz (2 lbs)	1 kg

Oven Temperatures

Heat	Fahrenheit	Centigrade/Celsius	British Gas Mark
Very cool	230	110	$1/4$
Cool or slow	275–300	135–150	1–2
Moderate	350	175	4
Hot	425	220	7
Very hot	450	230	8